MARTIAL ARTS SERIES

Karate
Techniques & Tactics

Patrick M. Hickey
Secretary, USA Karate Federation
7th-Dan Black Belt

Human Kinetics

Library of Congress Cataloging-in-Publication Data

Hickey, Patrick M.
    Karate techniques & tactics / Patrick Hickey.
        p.   cm. -- (Martial arts series)
    Includes bibliographical references and index.
    ISBN 0-88011-594-7
    1. Karate.   2. Karate--Training.   I. Title.   II. Series.
    GV1114.3.H534   1997
    796.815'3--dc21   96-37722
                                                                    CIP

ISBN: 0-88011-594-7

Acquisitions Editor: Kenneth Mange; **Developmental Editor:** Julie A. Marx; **Assistant
Editors:** Andrew Smith, Erin Cler, and Coree Schutter; **Editorial Assistant:** Jennifer
Hemphill; **Copyeditor:** Holly Gilly; **Proofreader:** Erin Cler; **Graphic Designer:** Robert
Reuther; **Graphic Artists:** Robert Reuther and Denise Lowry; **Photo Editor:** Boyd
LaFoon; **Cover Designer:** Jack Davis; **Cover and Interior Photographer:** Anthony
Onchak; **Illustrator:** Rob Csiki; **Printer:** United Graphics

Human Kinetics books are available at special discounts for bulk purchase. Special
editions or book excerpts can also be created to specification. For details, contact the
Special Sales Manager at Human Kinetics.

Printed in the United States of America   10   9   8   7   6   5   4   3   2   1

Human Kinetics
Web site: http://www.humankinetics.com/

United States: Human Kinetics, P.O. Box 5076, Champaign, IL 61825-5076
1-800-747-4457
e-mail: humank@hkusa.com

Canada: Human Kinetics, Box 24040, Windsor, ON N8Y 4Y9
1-800-465-7301 (in Canada only)
e-mail: humank@hkcanada.com

Europe: Human Kinetics, P.O. Box IW14, Leeds LS16 6TR, United Kingdom
(44) 1132 781708
e-mail: humank@hkeurope.com

Australia: Human Kinetics, 57A Price Avenue, Lower Mitcham, South Australia 5062
(08) 277 1555
e-mail: humank@hkaustralia.com

New Zealand: Human Kinetics, P.O. Box 105-231, Auckland 1
(09) 523 3462
e-mail: humank@hknewz.com

This book is dedicated to all the karate masters who came before me and to those who I will leave behind.

CONTENTS

Preface   vi

Acknowledgments   ix

CHAPTER 1   GETTING STARTED   1

CHAPTER 2   ROOTS OF KARATE   13

CHAPTER 3   LANGUAGE AND CUSTOMS
             OF KARATE   21

CHAPTER 4   STANCES, MOVEMENT,
             AND BREATHING   33

CHAPTER 5   BLOCKS, FALLS, AND ROLLS   57

CHAPTER 6   PUNCHES AND STRIKES   77

CHAPTER 7   KICKS AND SMASHES   101

CHAPTER 8   STRATEGIES AND TACTICS   127

CHAPTER 9   KATA   151

CHAPTER 10   KUMITE COMPETITION   163

CHAPTER 11   CONDITIONING   185

Suggested Readings   199

Index   201

About the Author   205

PREFACE

The Japanese martial art of karate has become an important and, for some, necessary part of growing up in today's society. Karate provides not only self-defense skills, but also the self-confidence, self-discipline, and self-control skills that are necessary to function in today's world. For many people, karate will provide the means to improve their general physical condition and to increase their strength, flexibility, and fitness. Through participation in sport activities, you will be able to safely and skillfully challenge your martial arts skills and test your mastery of these skills. In karate, these sport activities are called kumite (free-fighting) and kata (form) competition. This book will provide instruction on useful skills, concepts, techniques, tactics, and strategies that can help all martial artists improve their performance.

During the last few years, karate's popularity has greatly increased as people have recognized the invaluable skills that karate can provide. Movies and TV programs that feature karate reach into every home, making karate a rapidly growing part of the modern society in which we live. Who can participate in karate? Just about everyone can: from the 5-year-old kindergartner, to the high school or college student, to the 50-year-old professional. Young children practice karate because they get a thrill from discovering new and interesting things at their own pace. Parents like karate because it teaches discipline to their children. Martial arts are very popular in the late-teen and young-adult age groups, with karate classes offered for credit in many colleges and universities and in some high schools. Many people find that karate not only keeps them trim and fit, but also provides them with valuable self-defense skills.

The growth of karate throughout the world has been tremendous. Karate competition was first held in the Pan-American

Games in 1995. Karate also has been featured in the World Games, the Asian Pacific Games, the European Games, and the African Games. While this book deals with the sport aspects of karate, you do not have to be a tournament champion to participate in karate activity or to learn from this book. The techniques and examples described in this book work well for practice in the dojo (karate school). Many karate practitioners never enter a tournament, but this does not mean they cannot study and use the competition tactics of the champions.

Karate Techniques & Tactics was written with three audiences in mind: beginning, intermediate, and advanced karate practitioners. For the beginner, I introduce the value of karate. I explain karate's concepts, ideas, and vocabulary, and provide information on how to properly perform the various techniques. All of this information is necessary to learn karate. The intermediate student gains assistance in further understanding the use and practice of karate techniques and is introduced to more advanced concepts and ideas that will increase their skills. Included are the tactics, competition rules, and conditioning training used by successful karate practitioners. Advanced students who desire a deeper understanding of martial arts concepts and of their application in challenging circumstances will find this book an invaluable reference.

Chapter 1 explains how to find a karate school or instructor and describes the belt-ranking system used in karate. Chapter 2 covers the history of karate, the development of karate in the United States, and the development of karate sports competition. The vocabulary and terms that are used in karate training are included in chapter 3. Chapters 4 through 7 contain detailed descriptions of the stances, postures, attacks, and common defenses used in karate. Tactics and strategies are covered in chapter 8, which includes methods of moving the body for defense and power and explains how to use timing and speed to your advantage. Combinations, leg sweeps, and off-balancing as used by international champions are illustrated. Chapter 8 also provides an understanding of the psychologically opportune moment to attack. Chapters 9 and 10 cover kata (form) and kumite (free-fighting) competition in karate, including preparation for free-fighting and the rules commonly used in competition. In chapter 11, I discuss additional conditioning techniques that will sharpen the body as a weapon.

Within karate there are many different Ryu-ha (schools): Goju Ryu, Shito Ryu, Kwanmukan, Rengokai, Shotokan, Wasshin Ryu, and others. Each has its own style or system of karate, but all meet together in friendly, but furious, sports competition. This book deals with those generic techniques and tactics that are found in the majority of karate styles and systems and that are used by their champion karate players.

It is not necessary to participate in actual competition in order to enjoy kumite or to get value from this book. Karate practice can be one of the most fun and rewarding sport activities you can find. The majority of karate-ka (those who practice karate) never enter an actual competition, but practice in the dojo. The idea of sport in the dojo is not to win, but to be able to use the skill of a higher level of learning and to meet and conquer your own barriers. A dojo provides competition in an exciting, fun, and individually challenging atmosphere. The techniques and concepts presented in this book will be valuable to anyone participating in karate, whether that involves friendly sparring between friends, competition among classmates in the dojo, or participation in a major martial arts tournament.

ACKNOWLEDGMENTS

Karate Techniques & Tactics was written to assist you in your karate training. This is one way for me to repay the help I received in my karate career—by passing on to you what I have learned. I would like to thank certain individuals who have helped me. First, my instructor and mentor for over 25 years: George E. Anderson of Akron, Ohio. He has had one of the most interesting martial arts careers, having been a vice president of the World Karate Federation (WKF) and the head of both its Referee Council and Medical Council. He oversaw the introduction of karate into the Pan-American Games and the formation of the Pan-American Union of Karate Organizations. He was also a member of the United States Olympic Committee. Mr. Anderson opened the door for me to make many of my international connections, and his guidance has been invaluable.

Next I would like to thank Mr. Takayuki Mikami of Metairie, Louisiana. Mr. Mikami is one of the best and most knowledgeable practitioners ever produced by the Japan Karate Association. My association with him over the past 15 years has given me a deeper insight into what karate should be.

Hidy Ochiai of Vestal, New York, is another long-time acquaintance and karate master whose advice on the Japanese culture has helped me in many ways. Mr. Ochiai assisted me in writing the history and Japanese language section of this book.

There are three other individuals I would like to mention who have provided much help and encouragement along the way. Minobu Miki of San Diego, California, and Koji Sugimoto of Miami, Florida, are two long-time senior WKF officials who were in charge of the karate event at the 1995 Pan-American Games—the first year that karate took place there. They have made sure that I understand the rules used in international competition and that my officiating stays at its peak. Also, there is Masaharu

Sakimukai of Jacksonville, Florida—one of the most interesting and excellent karate masters with whom I have had the honor to be associated.

Finally, I would like to acknowledge those martial arts masters who I had the opportunity to know but who have passed away. Saduki Nakabayashi, 8th dan Kodokan Judo, was my esteemed judo instructor. Grand Master Robert A. Trias gave me the job of organizing the United States Karate Association Police Liaison. Masafume Suzuki founded the Seibukan, and I had the honor of attending his funeral in Japan. (Hiroyasu Kobayashi, head of the United States Seibukan, was my guide while I was in Japan.)

In studying karate you will meet many interesting people who will lend guidance. You will also find yourself guiding others. So while I cannot name everyone who I would like to acknowledge, I want them all to know that I appreciate their friendship.

I want my readers to know that as you study karate, you will gain a burden. That burden is your responsibility to pass on those lessons that you have learned from those who came before to those who will come after. Thus karate lives throughout the ages and your legacy will be part of that continuity.

CHAPTER

1

GETTING
STARTED

Most people know very little about martial arts when they decide to take karate. This chapter looks at what karate is and explains belt ranking and how rank is earned. This chapter will also help you make the right decision in selecting a karate school.

THE VALUE OF KARATE

Karate provides a structure that helps participants develop both physical and mental skills. These abilities include strength, flexibility, self-confidence, and concentration. Strong character development—not taught in many of today's institutions—is learned through karate. Physical and mental discipline, which karate cultivates, produces an exceptional person. At the same time, karate training can be fun, challenging, and rewarding.

Karate has something for everyone. For both men and women, it provides an opportunity to become physically fit and at the same time learn self-defense. Karate is a challenging way to remain fit and to continue athletic endeavors, whatever your age. The young learn the value of discipline, goal setting, and successful accomplishment. Some parents use karate to teach discipline which is sorely missing in the school systems. Teenagers and young adults can participate in a challenging sport, developing and retaining strength and flexibility that can be lost if left undeveloped or unused.

For those who participate in other sport activities, karate provides the necessary foundation of muscular, aerobic, and anaerobic fitness. Karate also enhances sport performance by emphasizing speed and strength. For those who lack self-esteem and self-confidence, karate can provide improvement in these areas.

Karate training requires no special equipment or abilities. Students are not compared to each other, and the pressure to excel that is found in team sports is not present. In karate, each person is allowed to progress in the way that best fits the desires and goals of that individual.

A karate class.

WHAT IS KARATE?

Once you have decided to train in karate, your next step is to look for a karate school. This task is not always as simple as it seems. In the yellow pages you can find a number of different schools that advertise many different types and combinations of martial arts. Furthermore, karate has become a generic word, and it is the art that strikes the imagination when talking about the martial arts. Thus many martial arts schools advertise karate when they really teach something else. Because of the many similarities among the arts, the untrained observer can see no apparent difference. So let's see what distinguishes karate from the other martial arts, so you can determine whether it is karate that you want to learn.

KARATE

Karate is a martial art that was developed in Okinawa, then imported to mainland Japan (see chapter 2). There are many different styles, or systems, of karate. Within the various arts are Ryu-ha (schools of karate) that practice a particular style. Since karate is very individualistic, each school will have distinguishing characteristics.

Karate consists primarily of striking, blocking, and kicking techniques that use the hands and feet. As a Japanese martial art, it includes many of the cultural aspects and values of the Japanese culture (see chapter 3). In the sports world, karate has kept the traditional concept of noncontact rules where blows are controlled and hard contact is avoided. The kata (forms) used in most karate schools are the older kata handed down from early karate masters.

TAEKWONDO AND KOREAN KARATE

Taekwondo is a Korean art of hand-and-foot fighting. Karate found its way into Korea during the Japanese occupation of that country around World War I, and its practice has continued ever since. Many of the taekwondo schools in the United States actually teach the style of karate that was derived during this occupation. Around 1964, Korean karate took the name taekwondo to express the Korean cultural heritage and to show that taekwondo is not a Japanese martial art.

Since 1964, taekwondo has adopted a form of contact-sport rules that allow the use of body armor and designed *poomse* for their forms practice. However, many of the traditional Korean karate instructors in the United States have not followed this change and still teach traditional Korean karate. Yet they, too, often refer to their art as taekwondo in order to indicate its Korean heritage. The competition regulations used for traditional Korean karate are very similar to the karate competition rules concept. However, they sometimes support the newer taekwondo sport activities because those competition rules have been accepted by the international sports world.

Like karate Ryu, there are also many different styles of taekwondo, called *kwons*. The main physical difference between Korean karate/taekwondo and Japanese karate is found in the emphasis on the feet over emphasis on the hands. Korean martial arts tend to use more extended kicking and circular or wheeling types of kicking actions, and some schools do not have a well-developed hand system. Japanese karate tends to be more rigid and linear, with stronger hand systems, lower stances, and tighter kicking, but there are numerous exceptions to these rules.

KUNG FU

Kung fu means "fist art" and refers to Chinese martial arts in general. These arts, of course, express the Chinese culture. Tai-chi Chuan, Hsing-i, Pa-kua, and Wu Shu are examples of Chinese martial arts styles. These arts are usually characterized by flowing movements or very low to high stances and circular movements. Styles from southern China tend to be more flowing and softer than those of northern China. You can see some influences in both Japanese and Korean martial arts arising out of the early exchange with mainland China (see chapter 2).

OTHER MARTIAL ARTS

There are many other types of martial arts. Judo is a Japanese martial art that developed from jujitsu. By eliminating certain types of technique and by concentrating on throwing and grappling one's opponent, judo has developed into a fighting style that is represented in Olympic competition. Its founder, Jigoro Kano, gave this art the name judo, which means "gentle way." By using balance, leverage, and momentum in a flexible and efficient manner, judo applies skill and timing rather than the use of brute force to throw one's opponent. The essence of judo was summed up by Kano in his two maxims. The first is the optimal use of mental and physical energy, and the second is mutual welfare and benefit. Although judo participants do practice some strikes and kicks, the emphasis is on techniques that use only throws and grapples. Because of this emphasis, there is very little similarity between judo and karate.

Jujitsu is a martial art that concentrates on joint locks, throwing, and grappling, as well as strikes and kicks. Jujitsu differs from judo in that it uses wrist locks and other joint-lock techniques not permitted in judo. While jujitsu employs throws and locks, it does not concentrate on the use of the hands and feet as weapons as intensely as karate. Both judo and jujitsu work well for law enforcement officers.

Aikido is a martial art derived from aiki-jitsu by Morihei Uyeshiba. This art uses joint-locking techniques to throw one's opponent and employs strikes to vital areas of the body. Uyeshiba included elements of philosophy, psychology, and dynamics in his art. The essence of aikido is that you must first lead your mind by your ki (life energy) and then lead your opponent's mind thus controlling his actions. Aikido does not apply brute force. Rather, it seeks to develop the spiritual self and to defeat the opponent by bringing your movements into balance with those of your opponent. Aikido has a number of sitting and standing techniques and can include the use of a sword, spear, or club. Each technique is taught by the master as you come to understand ki and how to use it.

Many martial arts have developed around the use of weapons. Kendo is Japanese fencing with bamboo swords, and iaido is the art of drawing the sword. Kobudo is associated with the use of certain implements and tools found in Okinawa during the time weapons were banned (see chapter 2). These weapons include bo, sai, tonfa, kama, nunchaku, and eku (see chapter 9 for a description of each weapon).

There are too many types of martial arts to mention, but the above list describes the most popular ones. Instructors today are commonly trained in more than one martial art form, and they may teach those arts separately or as part of a general karate class. This is especially true for jujitsu and kobudo.

A registration conference.

SELECTING A KARATE SCHOOL

Now, having some idea of what karate is and what karate is not, you can go about selecting a karate school. First, consider who is planning to take karate lessons. A school suitable for adults may not be suitable for children. You should watch a class or two and observe the interaction between the instructors and the students.

If you are considering classes for your child, what are your goals? If you want to instill discipline, choose a school that practices good discipline in a nonpunishing environment. Are the classes fun? If not, your child will not want to continue. On the other hand, if the instructor just plays with the kids, this would not serve your purpose. Perhaps the most important factor to consider is whether the instructor is a role model that you want your child to follow. Because karate instructors will leave a lasting impression on the development of your child, this may be the single most important point. Do not be swayed by an instructor's claims of prowess. Just because someone is an excellent tournament competitor does not make that person a good teacher or enable one to deal with children. Request that your child be allowed to take a class or two before you make a decision.

After the class(es), meet with the instructor for a registration conference. At this conference ask the instructor if your child is suited for karate training, how he feels karate training will help your child, and question him on how the school is run. If the answers to these questions are satisfactory to you, then you can feel comfortable registering your child for classes.

If you are looking for a school for yourself, you should watch a class to see whether the instructor emphasizes the approach you want. What is the atmosphere of the school? Do you fit in? If you are looking for personal development and physical fitness, a school that emphasizes competition will probably not be right for you. If you want to compete, do not enroll in a school that sends few students to tournaments. If your interest is weapons, seek an instructor who also teaches kobudo. Law enforcement personnel may want some type of jujitsu training in addition to karate. In other words, match your desires and goals with a school that has the type of people you feel comfortable with, at a cost that you can afford. If you intend to make karate a lifetime activity, you should find out about the school's national and international affiliations. These affiliations will be important if you desire to learn a traditional style of karate. They give you some idea as to how the school can further your long-term participation in martial arts.

You should also consider the method of payment required and what additional services the school may offer. Does it provide the use of weights, exercise equipment, heavy bags, and other equipment? Must you pay up front, or is there a payment plan? Some schools require you to sign an agreement to take lessons for a particular period of time. There are pros and cons to this type of arrangement. It is good in the sense that it allows the instructors to make plans for the future, because it ensures their income and gives them long-term stability. It also provides incentive for the students to attend classes. This type of agreement is bad, however, if it requires a large advance payment for a black-belt course that may never be completed or if the agreement calls for a commitment of more than one year. Be especially careful if the school sells the contract to a finance company that assumes the debt. On the other hand, if no agreement is required, students may find it easy to stop taking classes, and the school may not be on solid financial footing.

Tuition costs are not the only expenses involved in taking karate lessons and should not be the only measure of what school to join. Some schools may have testing and registration fees that exceed $1,000! Ask about the fees and expenses, and get them in writing. Other expenses will include the cost of sparring equipment, a karate uniform, and other mandatory items. These expenses should be reasonable and controllable.

KARATE BELTS

The belt-ranking system used in karate is a modification of the system first used in judo around the beginning of the twentieth century. Various colors of belts are used to measure progress in skill. These belts also serve as a reward system for setting and attaining goals and to indicate to the instructor where the students stand in their training. Levels below black belt are called kyu. There are various levels and belt colors associated with each

TABLE 1.1
One Karate Belt-Ranking System

Name	Belt	Level	Approximate minimum training time*
Jusankyu	White	13th kyu	Beginning student
Junikyu	Orange	12th kyu	2 months
Juichikyu	Orange	11th kyu	4 months
Jukyu	Yellow	10th kyu	6 months
Kukyu	Yellow	9th kyu	8 months
Hachikyu	Blue	8th kyu	10 months
Shichikyu	Blue	7th kyu	1 year
Rokyu	Green	6th kyu	14 months
Gokyu	Green	5th kyu	16 months
Yonkyu	Purple	4th kyu	20 months
Sankyu	Purple	3rd kyu	2 years
Nikyu	Brown	2nd kyu	28 months
Ikkyu	Brown	1st kyu	32 months

*Based on two 1-1/2-hour classes per week.

TABLE 1.2
Black Belt Levels and Training Times

Name	Level	Approximate minimum training time
Shodan	1st dan	3 years
Nidan	2nd dan	4 years
Sandan	3rd dan	6 years
Yodan	4th dan	9 years, age 30 and over*
Godan	5th dan	13 years, age 35 and over
Rokudan	6th dan	19 years, age 41 and over
Shichidan	7th dan	25 years, age 48 and over
Hachidan	8th dan	Age 58 and over, generally the leader of a style
Kudan	9th dan	Age 60 and over
Judan	10th dan	Age 70 and over

* Age requirements shown are those of the World Karate Federation.

kyu (see table 1.1). In general, black belt levels are called dan. There are 10 dan levels (see table 1.2).

While there are a number of different belt-color systems, the one used by most schools is white, green, brown, and black. Many systems supplement these colors by inserting additional colors between them or by putting stripes on the belts to indicate advancement. A common belt system today might have the colors in the following order: white, orange, yellow, blue, green, purple, brown, and black. The belt colors signify progressive levels of skill.

Understanding the ranking of the colors can be difficult. Not only can different schools that teach the same system vary in their use of colors, but different systems have different color rankings. Some karate systems refer to a yellow belt as a gold belt. Some Korean karate styles issue a red belt just before the brown belt, and at least one Korean system uses a dark blue belt in place of a black belt. Judo and jujitsu styles often use a red belt or a belt with alternating red and white sections to indicate high black-belt status. Chinese martial arts systems use sash colors that do not conform to the karate belt-ranking system.

Testing for belt rank.

BELT RANKS AND ADVANCEMENT

You will not need gymnastic flexibility and suppleness in order to move up in karate rank. Nor is it necessary to keep up with fancy techniques to earn a black belt. Reputable schools require only that their students reach a high level of understanding and that they learn proper karate technique according to their body's capabilities.

Basically, the belt system provides a means by which the instructor can rank students by levels of accomplishment and knowledge. There is no requirement for parity among different karate schools. That is why a student could be a black belt in one school but not in another. For example, I had a friend who had been a second-degree black belt for three years. One day he shared a kata (form) with a friend of his who had been a second-degree black belt for about a year. Ten days later, this person was promoted to third-degree black belt based on what he had learned from my friend.

Another example is a seven-year-old girl who came into my dojo with her dad to discuss taking classes. She had been training for only two years and was already a second-degree black belt! Now, I have taught many young people, and I have a good understanding of what a seven-year-old can do. This girl may have met the standard of her school, but most traditional schools do not operate in such a lenient manner. I happen to know that her instructor charged close to $1,000 for a black belt test. I often have wondered if the parents of this child were gullible enough to pay that amount of money because of the pride they felt over their daughter being considered to have such exceptional talent. In other words, was the child actually that good, or did the instructor take advantage of the parents?

In testing for belt rank, most schools measure your growth in understanding of karate and your physical and mental improvement since the last testing. Thus most tests will include a demonstration of improvement in karate kihon, which comprises the mechanical details and methods of performing karate techniques. This includes increased ability in balance, posture, coordination, speed, timing, control, and power. In addition, tests will require the performance of the required kata (form) for the next skill level and an understanding and use of karate technique both in prearranged fighting and free-fighting. Oral and written tests on vocabulary, history, and other concepts are also common. Attitude and effort in class between tests have an impact on which students will be allowed to attend the testing.

TIME IN GRADE

At below black-belt grades, promotions usually occur about every two to three months (see table 1.1). Most schools have one or two rank-levels for each colored belt. As students progress toward the higher grades, a period of three to four months between tests is not unusual. Much of the time spent in a grade depends on how much class time a student gets in and how much the student practices between classes. In most systems, it will take three to five years to progress to black belt. Black belts below a certain age are usually considered junior levels and are converted to adult rank after a certain age. It is not uncommon for some organizations to have an age limit for awarding higher black-belt grades. Normal timing for higher black-belt ranks depends on the rank level (see table 1.2). First-degree black belts can usually test for second-degree black belt after at least one year of training. Second-degrees can test for third-degree status after a minimum of two years and so forth. These are only guidelines, and there are many exceptions.

THE BLACK BELT

A black belt is someone who understands the requirements for a black belt and can perform them at the required level. A black belt has developed a maturity of karate movement. When you first enter a karate dojo and see a black belt, you assume that he must know a great deal about karate. Yet the best black belts are those

Receiving the coveted black belt.

who, after studying karate, have come to know what they do not know. Presumably they understand the requirements of the lower ranking levels, and in that sense they know everything that those who are beneath black-belt status know. In a larger sense, however, the black belt understands his limitations and possesses a devotion to study that will enable him to reach a higher level of understanding. In the dojo, black belts are treated with respect. This respect, however, is not given to the person just because he has become a black belt, but also because of the effort that the person put into achieving that status. Most black belts assume teaching duties in the dojo, thereby passing on what they have learned to the beginning students in addition to continuing their training for higher belt levels.

Karate can be of benefit to students of all ages who are interested in sharpening their mental and physical skills, including concentration, self-confidence, and overall fitness, not to mention their ability to defend themselves. Joining the correct karate school can be one of the most rewarding decisions a person can make, and reaching the black-belt level could be the most rewarding accomplishment you make in your lifetime. As you begin and continue with your karate training, knowledge of the history of karate and the language and customs you'll encounter in a typical karate class that I discuss in the following chapters will increase your appreciation and understanding of the art.

CHAPTER

2

ROOTS OF
KARATE

In the past, knowledge of karate history was generally passed down through oral tradition, from master to student. It was considered important to know one's roots. After all, how can anyone know where they are going if they do not know from where they came? This chapter gives a general history of karate and explains the standing of karate competition on the international level.

Modern karate originally was developed over several centuries by the people on the Ryukyu Islands. Its development was influenced by other cultures and areas, especially China. Kara-te originally was known as To-te, meaning "Chinese hands." The Chinese influence blended with the martial art known as Okinawan-te (Okinawan hands) to produce the karate we know today. Karate was introduced into Japan in 1922 and into the United States in 1945—less than one generation after it first appeared on mainland Japan.

DEVELOPMENT OF KARATE

Karate history goes back to the beginning history of man. The need to provide the basic necessities of food, shelter, and clothing required the ability to trap and kill wild animals. With some modification, these same skills also provided defense from wild animals and from bands of raiding people.

Those skills that were most effective were handed down to each new generation. Perhaps the earliest records in written history referring to martial arts are reports from the original Olympic games in Greece around 778 B.C. where mention is made of a hand strike that disabled a competitor. This event was known as the Pankration. Older records suggest a fighting system that was used in India. There is some debate as to whether Alexander the Great, in 327 B.C., may have exchanged fighting arts when he traveled to India. Some ancient statues depict various martial arts poses.

The spread of martial arts is attributed to Bodhidharma, a legendary monk who lived in the sixth century A.D. He is said to have crossed the Himalayas into China from India. He found the Chinese monks physically unfit from getting little exercise and spending many hours in seated meditation. Finding that their poor physical condition prevented proper meditation, Bodhidharma instituted a set of exercises based on fighting skills in order to improve the monks' fitness. Over time, these monks became the fiercest fighters in China.

OKINAWA

Around the fifteenth century, on a small group of islands called the Ryukyu Islands (Okinawa), the ruling Sho Dynasty confiscated all arms. This led to an interest in fighting with the hands, feet, and self-made weapons. Later, because merchant emissaries from China were replaced with military representatives, there was a renewed interest in fighting skills. The Okinawans combined their own fighting style known as te (hands) with the system that was brought over from China. This later became known as To-te, a Chinese style of self-defense. Additional interest in te occurred when the Satsuma clan from Japan conquered the Ryukyu Islands in the seventeenth century and banned the use of weapons. The ban lasted 300 years. Training passed down from father to son in secret. The art now known as karate began to take shape in the late seventeenth and early eighteenth centuries as te merged with the Chinese style of self-defense. This *te*, or Okinawan-te, combined with the Chinese influences to become known as "Kara-te" (Chinese hands).

Karate, however, did not become widely known until it was introduced in the Okinawan public schools in 1904 by Anko Itosu. Itosu created a series of karate exercises and called them the Pinan (later known as Heian in Japan) kata. These kata were adapted from the traditional kata formerly practiced in secret and were designed to make karate more acceptable for group instruction. These kata were first used in secondary schools in Okinawa for physical education.

JAPAN

It was not until 1922 that an Okinawan schoolteacher named Gichen Funakoshi was asked to give a demonstration of karate in Japan. The demonstration was successful, and Funakoshi was invited to stay and teach. Over time, other schools of karate sent teachers to Japan, and karate began its assimilation into the Japanese culture.

The introduction of karate in Japan came at a time of changing values. Japan had left the feudal period and entered early twentieth-century modern life. Warrior arts were of little use. For this reason, martial arts were changed and redefined. During this period, the Japanese characters for kara-te were changed to mean "empty hand," reflecting a spiritual concept rather than a mere fighting system. The zen concept of *do* (way) was combined with karate to produce the concept karate-do. This concept indicated that karate was also now a means for the character development necessary for success in life.

Karate was an immediate success on mainland Japan. In 1931, it was officially adopted by the Nippon Butoku Kai, an organization formed to identify and to systematize the martial arts of Japan. Around 1936, various styles of karate were recognized by the Butoku Kai. This resulted in the change of the meaning of karate to be "an empty-handed self-defense art" or "weaponless art of self-defense."

AFTER WORLD WAR II

Karate survived World War II and spread rapidly during the post-war period. During the American occupation of Japan, karate was one of the martial arts not banned by the American government. United States servicemen were exposed to karate and brought it back to their homeland. The earliest known American martial artist was Robert Trias, who in 1946 started the first U.S. karate school. In 1948, Trias formed the United States Karate Association (USKA), the first known karate organization in this country.

Also in 1948, the Japan Karate Association (JKA) was formed. During the early and mid-1950s, there was an attempt to further organize karate in Japan. Sport rules were based on regulations first formulated around 1934, and the first karate championships took place. Matches were held by the JKA, and various colleges had clubs. Two men who are remembered from this period are Takayuki Mikami and Hirokazu Kanazawa. They were college roommates who became best known for their famous match at the 1958 All Japan Championships. Their match went into five overtimes before Mikami was declared the winner.

MODERN HISTORY

Little was done to further organize karate until the 1964 Olympics, which were held in Japan. At that time, the Federation of All Japan Karate Organizations (FAJKO—now known as the Japan Karate Federation [JKF]) was formed.

In 1970, the FAJKO sent invitations to Japanese instructors throughout the world to attend a world championship in Tokyo, Japan. This invitation was in response to the need to develop a standardized set of competition rules and the need to have an international organization represent karate worldwide. The World Union of Karate-do Organizations (WUKO, known since 1993 as the World Karate Federation [WKF]) was established on October 14, 1970. Thirty-three countries attended this historical first world championship. The WUKO instituted a unified set of competition rules and judging system.

The first World Technical Congress was held under the WKF in 1983. This Technical Congress addressed many of the concerns of the coaches and referees in regard to the rule system that was in force. The competition rules for karate were restructured and redefined to provide a sound, traditional base for karate competition.

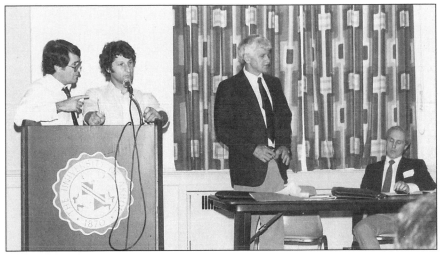

George Anderson presiding at the first World Technical Congress
of the World Karate Federation.

THE ATHLETIC TEST OF KARATE

Sport karate rewards courage, stamina, training, and technique. The original sport concept of karate was based on the idea of ippon (one killing blow) determining victory. Thus, the first competitor to execute a strike that could have "utterly cut down" the opponent if it was not controlled was declared the victor. This was called ippon shobu (one-strike match). Because one strike could cause victory, many karate players were very cautious and little display of technique was needed to win. For this reason, the matches were relatively unexciting. The first World Technical Congress, held in the United States in Akron, Ohio, in 1983 (and in which I was a representative from the United States) changed all this. The main decision arising from this meeting was the consensus among officials and coaches to change to a system in which three ippon, called sanbon in Japanese, were required for victory against an opponent. This change to shobu sanbon (three-ippon match) provides a system of rewards for technically difficult and exciting techniques. It also provides for a more exciting competition, while at the same time increasing the test of the athlete without breaking with the tradition of budo. Putting aside the concept of one killing blow solved the problems caused by a single-technique victory. Karate competition was put on a solid footing for expansion into major sports events.

These rules were subsequently adopted by the WKF. An explanation of the rules was compiled as an adjunct to the written regulations. Besides redrafting the rules of competition, the Technical Congress redefined the role that competition played in the karate martial art. The sport of karate was declared to be part of, rather than separate from, budo (the way of the warrior), upon which the martial arts were based. The Technical Congress determined that sport karate does not destroy the underlying concepts of budo, but is a sport system that keeps the traditional values of budo. These rules remain essentially unaltered and are still in use today at major international tournaments. Those competitions include the World Games, the Pan-American Games, and other continental contests.

WORLD KARATE FEDERATION

The WUKO changed its name in 1993 to the World Karate Federation (WKF). In 1976, the General Assembly of International Sports Federations (GAISF) recognized WKF as an international sports federation, and karate appeared in the first World Games in 1981. In 1985, the International Olympic Committee formally recognized WKF as the international governing body for sport karate in the world. WKF is now made up of nationally represented karate federations of all countries. It operates without favoritism toward any particular political or religious belief or style of karate. Over 130 nations are members of the WKF, and it is estimated that more than 100 million people in the world practice karate.

Ryoichi Sasagawa, the president of the World Karate Federation, presiding at the World Championships in Sydney, Australia.

PRIMARY STYLES OF KARATE IN THE WORLD KARATE FEDERATION

When the WKF was formed, the following four major karate styles provided the international framework for the organization:

- Shotokan, a term used by the followers of Gichen Funakoshi. Shoto means "pine tree" and kan means "house" or "place." Funakoshi, who used the term Shotokan for his calligraphy, is considered to be the father of karate in Japan. This style is supported by the Japan Karate Association.
- Wado Ryu, founded by Hironori Otsuka. The name means "way of peace" in the belief that the basis for the martial way is the way of peace.
- Goju Ryu, founded by Chojun Miyagusuku. The name comes from the Japanese words goken (strong fist) and juken (soft fist).
- Shito Ryu, founded by Kenwa Mabuni. The name comes from the Japanese characters of the karate masters Itosu and Higaonna, who were his instructors.

The premier competition in karate is the WKF World Championships, which are held every two years in different countries and on different continents. The best karate competitors from throughout the world, selected by the recognized Olympic sports body in each country, compete at this prestigious international event. Karate entered the World Games in 1981, and numerous World Cup competitions, including international collegiate and junior competitions have taken place. Karate now appears in all of the Continental Games, and discussion continues about how to get karate included in the Olympic Games. At this writing, the Olympic Committee is trying to limit participation in the Games to 10,000 athletes, making the introduction of new sports difficult, even though karate is now the third largest sport in the world.

KARATE IN THE UNITED STATES TODAY

In the United States now, there are many karate organizations. Many of these organizations are built around a particular style of karate or prominent karate master. They tend to have their own rules, but some follow the general direction of the international

Delegates to the first World Technical Congress from
Europe, Asia, North and South America, and the Pacific Rim.

sports world. Among the most noted of these organizations are the
United States Karate Kai, United States Karate Alliance, American Amateur Karate Federation, Gojuryu Karate-do Kai,
Kwanmukan International, and the International Shotokan Karate Association. Some, like NASKA (North American Sport
Karate Association), are very large and have a wide sports network
outside of the international karate sports network of the WKF.

Among those organizations that follow the WKF international
rules, three stand out. First is the USA Karate Federation, which
has operated as the national governing body for karate in the
United States for over 16 years. Next is the Amateur Athletic
Union, which has run karate sports for over 22 years and which
gave birth to The USA Karate Federation. Finally, there is the
USA National Karate-do Federation, which separated from the
USA Karate Federation and now operates as the current national
governing body for sports karate. These three organizations serve
as sources for accepted international karate sports standards.

The future of karate as an exciting international sport is very
bright because karate has entered all the continental games. Its
way to the Olympics will be rough because of the International
Olympic Committee's limit on participation in the Olympic Games
and the competing interests of other international sports. In any
event, the popularity of karate is increasing daily, as more and
more people realize the benefits of karate training.

CHAPTER

3

LANGUAGE AND CUSTOMS OF KARATE

Karate, as a Japanese art, uses many terms, phrases, and traditions from the Japanese culture. Every karate practitioner has some knowledge of the meaning and use of the Japanese terms. Some of the more esoteric terms have no exact English equivalent, and the Japanese word is used to convey the meaning.

The following rules provide a guide as to how to pronounce the Japanese words correctly. Japanese vowels sound more like the vowels in Spanish than in English. Japanese long vowels are lengthened when pronounced. To guide your pronunciation, in this chapter long vowels are shown with a bar above each vowel in the first appearance of each Japanese term containing long vowels. A vowel between voiceless consonants (*p, t, k, ch, f, h, s, sh*)

or a vowel following a voiceless consonant at the end of the word
is not pronounced. Japanese consonants are similar to those in
English except that the g is always hard, except in ng. The s is
hissed. To pronounce the r, lightly touch your tongue to the ridge
of your mouth behind the top teeth; for the f, blow out air lightly
as if you were just beginning to whistle. Be aware that doubling
a Japanese consonant changes the meaning of a word. Do not
pronounce the consonant twice—instead, hold the sound longer.
Failure to follow these rules can change the meaning of a word
when pronounced or make it unintelligible.

For an example of Japanese pronunciation, karate is pronounced *kah-rah-teh*. The word shizen tai is pronounced *she-zen
tah-ee*. Mae-geri is *mah-eh geh-rhee*.

GENERAL TERMS

Karate-ka are those who study karate. The training hall for
karate is called the karate ***dōjō***. Often, there is a group of affiliated
karate dojos under one master instructor. The main dojo is
referred to as the ***Hombu dojo***. Styles of karate are called
Ryū.

The instructor at the karate school is called the ***sensei***. Other
words are also used for the word "instructor." Usually the head
instructor of a group of schools is known as ***shihan***. A ***sempai*** is
a student of higher rank but who is not a sensei or a shihan. ***Cohai***
are those students at the same rank. Black-belt ranks are referred
to as ***dan*** grades, and the ranks below black belt are called ***kyū***
levels.

A ***gi*** is the uniform worn during karate class. In most karate
schools, the participants wear a white gi. The gi consists of
gussetted pants that allow for freedom of movement and a loose-
fitting jacket tied at the sides. The jacket is further held closed by
an ***obi*** (belt) wrapped around the body and tied in a square knot.
Should a gi need adjusting during class, the karate-ka is expected
to turn and face the rear of the workout area before fixing the gi.
Shoes are not worn during class, nor are jewelry and other items
that can be a hazard.

Karate-ka bow when entering or leaving the karate dojo. This
bow, called ***rei*** in Japanese, is performed by respectfully bending
at the hips, keeping the eyes forward. Bowing is both a greeting

and a sign of respect. Karate-ka may also bow when entering or leaving the workout area or when addressing a karate-ka of higher rank.

The front of the workout area is called the ***shōmen*** and the rear, the ***shimoza***. In the front center is the ***shinzen*** (place of honor). This is the direction the karate-ka face when they bow to start class or when entering or leaving the dojo. Most schools will have a picture of the founder of their style, a ***kamiza*** (shrine), or the flag of their country in the place of honor.

The karate students should follow common courtesies in the dojo. Standing at attention when the instructor enters a room, carrying the instructor's bag or equipment, opening the door when he enters, and introducing oneself to new students are proper behaviors for the karate-ka. The karate-ka are also careful not to use their hands in order to sit or to rise.

Some schools practice greeting and saying good-bye in Japanese. A common greeting when entering the dojo would be ***"Onegai shimasu"*** ("I beg for your teaching"). This is a symbolic gesture to the sensei and to the dojo, humbly submitting yourself to be taught. Similarly, ***"Arigato, gozaimashita"*** for "Thank you" more literally means "I truly appreciate what I have been taught."

Proper courtesy is important in the karate dojo.

KARATE CLASS

Karate classes are very formal affairs. What follows is a general description of a karate class workout. Each school will have their own particulars and emphases, but the discussion below will teach you what to expect.

STARTING CLASS

There are many variations in traditions for lining up and starting class. Classes usually begin with the command *"Narande"* ("Line up"). Students go to their place in line, with the higher-ranking students up front. The *dai sempai* (highest-ranking student) is on the right, facing the shomen. All the other students line up to the left of the dai sempai in order of rank. Those who are the same rank line up in order of seniority. If two or more individuals have been training for the same period of time, the eldest lines up on the right. As a courtesy, the karate-ka allow visitors to line up ahead of them. At the end of the line are those who are not in full uniform because they have forgotten all or part of their gi.

If a second row is needed, it will start directly behind the senior student and continue to the left, with each student directly behind someone in the front row. In the lineup, the rows and columns must be straight, with enough space left between and in front of each student so that the workout can be conducted safely. It is the duty of the senior student to see that the lineup is correct.

Late-arriving students must wait at the side of the workout area until acknowledged by the instructor or senior student. When they are signaled to line up, they must go to the end of the line. Only when the line re-forms after a break in the class will they be allowed to resume their proper places.

The instructor calls the students to attention with the command *"Kiotsuke!"* ("Attention"). The commands for rei are then given: *"Shomen ni rei"* ("Bow to the front") and *"Sensei ni rei"* ("Bow to the instructor"). In most schools, when a higher ranking instructor enters the workout area, the first student to notice calls the class to attention and directs a rei toward that instructor. Some schools will sit in a *seiza* (Japanese sitting posture on the knees) and perform the rei from this position. Other schools will first issue the command *"Mokuso"* (pronounced muks so). Mokuso means "Close your eyes." The students close their eyes and meditate for a few minutes, relaxing and attuning their minds before beginning class.

Mokuso—quiet contemplation.

TRAINING TERMS

The instructor will use various commands during class. *"Yōi"* means "Get ready to begin," *"Hajime"* means "Begin," and *"Yame"* means "Immediately stop what you are doing and come to attention." Sometimes the teacher will use the word *"Matte."* This means "Be quiet and pay attention." A *kiai* is a shout or "spirit yell." A list of the Japanese terms for the techniques highlighted in this book, as well as for other common karate terms, is included at the end of this chapter.

During class, the commands are usually given by the instructor, followed by a kiai from the instructor that signals the student to follow the command. The student usually acknowledges the teacher's instructions or commands with the exclamation *"Hai!"* or *"Osu!"* meaning "Yes, I understand." When the teacher gives an instruction or command to an individual, the student accompanies the acknowledgment of the instruction or command with a bow.

It is common for the instructor to count the techniques and for the student to echo that count. Breathing correctly is important, and counting out loud makes it difficult to breathe incorrectly or to hold one's breath. The count is usually done in Japanese. Table 3.1 provides a list of the Japanese numbers for digits, tens, hundreds, and thousands. Numbers are formed similarly to the way they are in English. For example, in English, the number 321 comprises three hundreds, two tens (twenty), and a one. In Japanese, this number is sanhyaku (three hundreds) niju (two tens) ichi (one).

TABLE 3.1
Japanese Numbers

Digits		Tens		Hundreds		Thousands	
1	Ichi	10	Ju	100	Hyaku	1,000	Sen
2	Ni	20	Niju	200	Nihyaku	2,000	Nisen
3	San	30	Sanju	300	Sanhyaku	3,000	Sansen
4	Shi/yon	40	Yonju	400	Yonhyaku	4,000	Yonsen
5	Go	50	Goju	500	Gohyaku	5,000	Gosen
6	Roku	60	Rokuju	600	Rokuhyaku	6,000	Rokusen
7	Shichi/nana	70	Shichiju	700	Nanahyaku	7,000	Nanasen
8	Hachi	80	Hachiju	800	Hachihyaku	8,000	Hachisen
9	Ku	90	Kuju	900	Kuhyaku	9,000	Kusen

PRACTICE METHODS

Various practice methods are used in the study of karate. **Kihon** refers to the proper method of performing a technique used in karate. **Waza** is the general term for techniques. **Kata** practice is the study of traditional fighting forms that were designed by the original karate masters. **Kumite** represents the various ways to practice fighting.

Kata. Kihon kata are specific practice forms of a particular school designed to teach the "basics." Formal kata are the traditional practice forms handed down by the karate masters. Each of the formal kata has its own name and meaning, and various styles use different kata or variations of the same kata. Just a few of the common kata practiced are the Heian series, Tekki series, Bassai Sho and Dai, Saifa, Seienchen, San Sei Ru, Shi So Chin, and Sei Pai.

Kata is an individualistic practice method. Kata can be practiced anywhere or anytime and does not require any special equipment. Each kata has a special interpretation. **Bunkai** (analysis), however, is a special type of kata practice in which the kata movements are performed against attackers, demonstrating the meaning of the movements. (See chapter 9 for more information on kata performance.)

Kumite. There are a number of different methods used to practice kumite (free-fighting). These methods can involve anything from predefined attack-and-defense practice to free-moving attacking and defending. Each has its particular value.

Ippon kumite is controlled, one-step fighting. A prearranged attack is made, sometimes upon a signal from the instructor, and a predetermined defense is executed. This defense can involve one or more techniques in combination. Sometimes the practice is performed in a fighting stance and at other times from an open-leg stance. Usually the *uke* (attacker) steps back with a kiai, signaling readiness to attack. When he is ready, the *tori* (defender) uses a kiai to signal the uke to attack. As karate-ka become advanced, the uke may attack without a signal.

Semi-free ippon kumite is similar to ippon kumite except that fighting stances are used, and either the defender or the attacker is given some freedom in movement. The participants can also use their judgment in the selection and timing of the techniques. *Sanbon* and *gohan kumite* are similar to ippon kumite except that three or five attacks are made before the defense is executed. *Jiju kumite* is free-fighting in which students freely attack and defend against each other in a controlled environment governed by a set of rules to prevent injury. (See chapter 8 for a more detailed look at jiju kumite.)

Practicing the bunkai (interpretation) of the Bassai Dai kata "Penetrating the Fortress."

THE KARATE WORKOUT

Most karate workouts follow a general pattern. They usually begin with five to ten minutes of *jumbi undo* (warm-up) exercises with some *yobi undo* (stretching). This is followed by 20 to 30 minutes of drill work or kihon (basic technique) practice. Line drills (moving back and forth) and kihon kata are commonly used, either singularly or in combination, to perfect blocks, strikes, and kicks. Correct stances are emphasized. This part of the class can move along at a very aerobic pace. A cool-down period and stretching usually follow this part of class.

Next, the workout usually consists of waza (technique) practice with a partner. Controlled forms of kumite, *goshin-jitsu* (self-defense), and other similar skills are introduced, practiced and perfected. During this part of class, it is not enough just to practice defensive technique. It is also important that the student concentrate on being a good partner by attacking correctly, not flinching, and learning how to work with someone else. If a student attacks incorrectly, she can unintentionally force her partner to practice incorrect technique.

The next part of the workout usually involves kata practice. Lower-ranking kata is usually practiced as a group, whereas higher-ranking kata is practiced individually or in smaller groups. Jiju kumite (free-fighting) usually rounds out the class. This part of the workout should end with additional stretching.

ENDING CLASS

After the workout, a formal procedure is followed, usually similar to the way class had started. The instructor may call "Mukoso." After a brief meditation, the students may bow from a standing or seiza position, and the class will be dismissed. The advanced students usually leave the floor first, followed by the lower-ranking students. In some schools, the higher-ranking students line up at the side of the workout area, and the lower-ranking students individually bow and thank the higher ranks as they leave the training area.

Because karate is a Japanese martial art, knowledge of the Japanese terms and commands is essential to be able to participate fully. Furthermore, most high-level events are officiated in Japanese (see chapters 9 and 10). Some words used in karate have no real English equivalent, again making an understanding of the Japanese language necessary.

Finally, following protocol in karate is extremely important. Senior karate instructors will evaluate you not just on the basis of your technique, but also on the basis of your courtesy. Closely following the rules and protocol in the dojo also provides for safe training and helps create the proper atmosphere for learning.

STANCES (TACHI)

Japanese	English
fudō-dachi	rooted stance
kiba-dachi	straddle-leg stance
kokutsu-dachi	back stance
kōsa-dachi	X-stance
neko-ashi-dachi	cat stance
sanchin-dachi	hourglass stance
shiko-dachi	square or sumo stance
shizen tai	natural body posture
hachiji-dachi	open-leg stance
heisoku-dachi	parallel stance (heels and toes together)
musubi-dachi	attention stance (heels together, toes turned out)
reinoji-dachi	L-stance
teiji-dachi	T-stance
zenkutsu-dachi	front stance

BLOCKS (UKE)

Japanese	English
age-uke	rising block
gedan barai-uke	downward block
jodan-uke	upper block
jūji-uke	X-block
kakiwake-uke	wedge block
morote-uke	two-handed/supporting block
shutō-uke	knife-hand block

soto-ude-uke	outside-inside arm block
uchi-ude-uke	inside-outside arm block
wantō-uke	sword-arm block

PUNCHES (*TSUKI*)

Japanese	English
choku-tsuki	straight punch
dan-tsuki	double punch
gyaku-tsuki	reverse punch
hasami-tsuki	scissors punch
heiko-tsuki	parallel punch
morote-tsuki	both-hands punch
oi-tsuki	lunge punch
ren-tsuki	alternate punch
sonoba-tsuki	basic punch
age-tsuki	upper punch
awase-tsuki	U-punch, arms close together
kagi-tsuki	hooking punch
mawashi-tsuki	roundhouse punch
tate-tsuki	upward punch
ura-tsuki	"close" punch
yama-tsuki	wide U-punch, arms apart (mountain strike)

STRIKES (*UCHI*) AND HAND POSITIONS

Japanese	English
haishu	backhand/backhand strike
haitō	ridge hand/ ridge-hand strike
hiraken	flat fist/fore-knuckle fist
ippon-ken	one-knuckle fist
kakutō	bent wrist/bent-wrist strike
keitō	chicken wrist/chicken-wrist strike
kentsui or *(tettsui)*	hammer fist/hammer-fist strike/bottom fist

kumade	bear hand/bear-hand strike
nakadaka-ken	middle finger one-knuckle fist
nukite	spear hand
seiken	forefist
seiryutō	ox jaw/ox-jaw strike
shutō / shutō-uchi	knife hand/knife-hand strike
soto mawashi-uchi	outside circular strike
tate-uchi	vertical strike
teishō	palm heel/palm-heel strike
mawashi-uchi	inside circular strike
uraken	back of fist/backfist strike
washide	eagle hand/eagle-hand strike
yoko-uchi	sideways strike

KICKS (KERI)

Japanese	English
gyaku mikazuki-geri	reverse crescent kick
keage	snap kick
kekomi	thrust kick
mae-geri	front kick
mawashi-geri	roundhouse kick
mikazuki-geri	crescent kick
nidan-geri	double kick
tobi-geri	jump kick
ushiro-geri	back kick
yoko-geri	side kick

SMASHES (ATE)

Japanese	English
empi-ate	elbow smash
hiza-ate	knee smash

STRIKING SURFACES

Japanese	English
ashi	foot
hiza	knee
kakato	heel
koshi	ball of foot
te	hand
sokutō	side edge of heel/sword foot
ude	arm

DIRECTIONAL TERMS

Japanese	English
age	rising
barai	sweeping
chūdan	middle
gedan	lower
gyaku	reverse
hanmi	side facing
hidari	left
jōdan	high/upper
kake	hook
mae	forward
mawashi	round
migi	right
otoshi	downward
tate	vertical/upward
tobi	jump
ushiro	backward
yoko	sideward

CHAPTER

4

STANCES, MOVEMENT, AND BREATHING

S wift and powerful karate requires proper kihon (basic technique). Each punch, kick, strike, or block must have good form (katachi). In order to apply maximum force at the moment of impact, proper stances must support these actions.

Maximum power comes from coordinating the entire body, mind, and spirit, thereby eliminating unnecessary motion so nothing is wasted, nothing withheld. Karate masters control the expansion and contraction of their muscles in order to execute the explosive movements of the hips that provide awesome power. They use only those muscles needed for a specific technique, moving them in the correct order to increase speed and to extend stamina. The practitioner's choice of rhythm and timing determines the swiftness or slowness of the action. Balance, stability, rhythmic order of movements, controlled breathing, and proper flow of the muscles can only come about through training in the correct karate kihon.

STANCES

Karate stances can be divided into two aspects: tachi and kamae. Tachi means "stance" and pertains to the lower part of the body. Kamae refers to the posture of the upper part of the body. Stances are important because they provide the support base for all karate techniques. Stances in themselves do not create power. It is the movement within the stance or from stance to stance that provides the dynamics for force. No matter how well you perform your blocks, punches, strikes, and kicks, these techniques will be weak and ineffective if you do not use the correct stances.

In karate it is possible for the same stance to be either straight or reverse. The word *straight* refers to the front of the body and the word *reverse* to the back of the body. For example, a reverse punch (gyaku-tsuki) is a punch with the hand that corresponds with the back leg. Similarly, a straight punch (choku-tsuki) uses the arm over the forward foot. In a stance, a straight position uses the forward arm as a guard over the front leg. A reverse stance uses the arm corresponding to the back leg as the guard. Thus the phrase "reverse stance." The word hanmi means the hips are side-facing in a stance—that is, one hip is forward of the other. When they are in a reverse side-facing position, the phrase gyaku hanmi is used.

The height of a stance is determined by the height of the hips. As the hips rise, the center of mass of the body rises giving more mobility but reduces stability. The lower the hips, the more stable the stance, but mobility is sacrificed. Generally speaking, the lower the stance, the more stable; the higher the stance, the more mobile. To block a strong attack, a strong stance, such as a back stance, is needed. Yet you would use a lighter stance, like the cat stance, to avoid the contact altogether. Most stances have a strong direction and a weak direction. Understanding the strong and weak points of the stance can be very useful in developing both offensive and defensive tactics: Attack to the weakness in a stance, defend in the strong position of the stance.

Straight hanmi.

Reverse hanmi.

WALKING THROUGH THE STANCES

The best way to see how the various stances relate is to try this exercise. Start in a straddle-leg stance. Without changing the distance between the feet, rotate on the middle of the feet (not the ball or heel) into a front stance. Shift the back knee to its original position, and transfer the weight over the back leg, forming a back stance. Pull the forward foot back, and turn the back leg into the position it was in for the front stance to form a cat stance. Twist the body 180 degrees to form an X-stance. Throughout these movements, do not raise your hips. Your knees and ankles should remain strong, bending or straightening as needed to accommodate the stance. Once you have completed the above pattern, reverse the order back to a straddle-leg stance and then practice the other side.

TECHNIQUE TIPS—STANCES

1. Keep the knees and ankles strong, gripping the floor with the toes.
2. The knees should be directly over the toes and both the knee and toe should point in the same direction.
3. Keep the proper stress by pushing the knees outward or inward as the stance requires.
4. When stressing the knees outward, push them toward the little toe.
5. Study and understand the correct weight displacement in each stance.
6. Except for the forward foot in a cat stance or the rear foot in an X-stance, keep the soles of the feet flat on the floor.
7. When shifting in a stance or moving between stances, keep the hips moving on a level plane, absorbing the motion in the knees and ankles.
8. Each stance has advantages and disadvantages. Learn the best way to use each stance.
9. Unless your style uses a leaning stance, keep the upper body erect, with the spine straight. The hips remain level, and the shoulders stay in place, even and relaxed.

NATURAL BODY POSITIONS

Shizen tai is the natural posture of the body. You generally will use five natural body positions in karate:

- Hachiji-dachi (open-leg stance)
- Teiji-dachi (T-stance)
- Reinoji-dachi (L-stance)
- Musubi-dachi (attention stance, heels together and toes turned out)
- Heisoku-dachi (parallel stance, heels and toes together)

All the natural stances maintain a heightened sense of alertness, ready to move in an instant. The legs are generally relaxed, but a slight tension is maintained about the joints.

The open-leg stance is an eight-direction stance. From this position the body can move quickly in one of eight directions: front or back, left or right, left front, right front, left back, and right back. This stance positions you to quickly attack or defend. In the T-stance, the feet form a T on the floor. In the L-stance, they form a loosely shaped L. In the T-stance and the L-stance either foot can be forward, with the body turned away from the direction you are facing. These last two stances are excellent defensive positions. The attention and parallel stances are not fighting stances but are used for training and class structure.

Open-leg stance.

T-stance.

L-stance.

Attention stance.

Parallel stance.

FRONT STANCE

For the zenkutsu-dachi (front stance), bend the front leg to an extent that when you look over the front knee, you can barely see the tips of your toes. Distribute your weight so that 60 to 70 percent rests on the front leg. In this stance, the feet are one shoulder-width apart from one side to the other, and about two shoulder-widths apart from the front to the back of the stance. The torso can be facing ahead or to the side. For most blocks you will face slightly to the side; for strikes, you will turn the torso forward, but there are exceptions. Whichever position you use, face in the direction of the stance. Point the front foot straight ahead, and turn the back foot as far forward as possible, but not to the point that the heel comes off the floor. Keep outward tension on the front knee, directed over the little toe, and press the back leg forward without locking the knee. A front stance is extremely strong in the forward direction. At an angle, however, the little finger can easily off balance the strongest person. This is an excellent stance to move into as you attack forward.

BACK STANCE

To achieve the kokutsu-dachi (back stance), point one foot straight ahead, and turn the other 90 degrees to the side. Distribute your weight 60 to 70 percent on the back leg, almost as if sitting on that leg. Press both knees outward, and turn your body to the side. The imaginary line that stretches from one heel to the other goes in the direction of the stance. This position is very strong to the front; you can use it for blocking or for launching powerful attacks.

STRADDLE-LEG STANCE

For the kiba-dachi (straddle-leg stance), spread your feet in a straight line about two shoulder-widths apart and point your feet straight ahead. Gripping the floor with the toes, lower your hips directly downward by bending your knees forward of the ankles and keeping your back straight. Press your knees outward. This is a basic training stance that develops powerful legs, hips, and ankles. As a fighting stance, use only for fighting to the side. Because it resembles the position of a rider on horseback, this stance sometimes is called a horse-riding stance.

HOURGLASS STANCE

To execute the sanchin-dachi (hourglass stance), put the heel of one foot and the ball of the other foot on a horizontal line about the width of your shoulders. Turn the forward foot inward and point the back foot straight ahead. Bend your legs until your knees touch. Strongly tighten your buttocks while pulling your inside thigh muscles together and gripping the floor with your toes. This will cause your knees to separate slightly. Keep your upper body erect. Be careful not to tip the pelvis too far forward or backward but to center it over the stance. This is a very strong position for blocking and striking, but it is not a very mobile stance.

SQUARE OR SUMO STANCE

Shiko-dachi (square or sumo stance) looks similar to the straddle-leg stance except that you point your feet about 45 degrees to the side. The difference is that your weight settles downward as you bend your knees over your feet. In this stance, the feet are often set at a 45-degree angle to the direction of the movement. This is a very strong stance for defending against side attacks.

CAT STANCE

In the neko-ashi-dachi (cat stance), support your weight on the rear foot and point it about 45 degrees to the side. Bend at the knees and ankles until the height of the hips is approximate to the height of the hips in the other stances. (For this, you will need to bend your knees and ankles farther then usual.) When you put most of your weight on your rear leg, your other leg will drop at the knee and be positioned on the ball of your foot. In most styles of karate, the hips face straight ahead in this stance but are tucked in, ready to spring forward like a cat from a crouch. In other styles, you will position your hips sideways when blocking and turn them forward when attacking. In more exaggerated poses, your forward ankle is locked downward and your toes are curled up. In other styles, your toes will be pointed downward. Use cat stances for quick blocking and attacking and for springing out of the way.

X-STANCE

To achieve the kosa-dachi (X-stance), put all of your weight on one foot. To balance yourself, cross your other foot in front of or behind the weight-bearing foot. This stance often is used when landing from a high jump or when side-stepping.

ROOTED STANCE

As its name implies, the fudo-dachi (rooted stance) is a very strong, fixed stance. To achieve this stance, first position yourself in a side-facing front stance. Now rotate your body into a straddle-leg stance. Keeping your feet in place and distributing your weight equally, turn your hips back to their original position. Maintain outward tension by pushing the knees out over the outside of the foot. This is a strong stance for defense.

Upper-Body Position

Kamae is the position of the upper body. This position generally follows the principles of good posture (although some styles use a leaning position of the upper body). Keep your spine and head erect and direct your gaze toward the front of the stance. Relax and balance your shoulders; neither shoulder should be higher than the other. Reverse or straight kamae can be used.

Various stances may employ different upper-body positions. It would be impossible to explain all the possible variations of kamae. Most of the differences lie in the placement of the arms and formation of the hands. The most popular hand forms are the fist and knife hands, but other hand forms can be used (see chapter 6). The idea is to keep the arms in a protective or menacing manner, exhibiting no opening for attack. Three common guards are described and illustrated on the following pages.

Practice of kamae includes the practice of zanshin—literally "remaining mind." Your mind must be ready to act, without interference, to the circumstances at hand. It receives input (perception) through the senses, primarily through your eyes. Your eyes must not stare at any specific part of your opponent's body, but rather "look through" your rival on the path that a strike would follow if it where extended. Center your gaze on the imaginary line between your adversary's shoulders. With your vision fixed in this way, you will be able to sense, rather than observe, your opponent's eyes, and your peripheral vision will pick up any movement of the extremities.

MIDDLE GUARD

The middle guard is the most common guard position. As in most fighting positions, your body faces to the side. On your forward arm, hold the elbow about a fist's distance away from your body, and position your hand in front of the opposite shoulder. Your elbow should be near one side of the body and your fist near the other side. Hold the hand of your nonguarding arm in a position that protects your solar plexus, palm up. The line from your elbow to your wrist cuts through your forward arm near its wrist, pointing directly at the target. If your rear arm is in a knife-hand position, your hand would be parallel to the floor. The elbow would be slightly below the hand so that the arm angles upward.

LOW GUARD

This guard is similar to the middle guard, except that your forward-arm hand will be slightly below the height of the hips.

HIGH GUARD

To achieve the basic high-guard position, place the upper part of your forward arm parallel to the ground and position the lower part of that arm perpendicular to the ground. Expand your chest and contract your back so that the arm is held along the forward side of your body and out of your line of sight. Hold your rear arm with its palm side out, with the knuckles near your temple. Hold the upper part of this arm perpendicular to the ground and position the lower part parallel to the floor. It is also acceptable in the various guard positions to hold the arms at two different levels, such as one low and one high.

MOVEMENT

For your karate techniques to be powerful, you must understand the dynamics of body movement. Create dynamic action by moving within the stance or between stances. Motion within a stance usually involves moving your hips from the side-facing position to the forward facing position and then back. Movement between stances usually results from a change of position from defensive to offensive. However, this motion can involve a series of offensive or defensive actions. No matter what moves you make, the important aspects will be the same. For each movement there is a pivot (or driving) leg and a moving (or attacking) leg. The pivot leg powers the strike. The moving leg provides balance and stability and affects the timing of the attack. You can also use the moving leg to attack, as with a kick.

In order for a karate technique to have maximum effect, the various parts of your body must support each other. The *connections* are where the joints come together: the wrist to the forearm, the forearm to the upper arm, the upper arm to the shoulder, the shoulder to the trunk, the trunk to the hip, the hip to the thigh, the thigh to the lower leg, and the lower leg to the foot. These connections, which the muscles strongly support at the instant of contact, work together to drive the full force of the karate blow into the target. If any muscle contracts at the wrong moment or if a connection is lined up too early or too late, the whole body weakens, and the effectiveness of the karate blow is lost.

Strength and speed generate power. Speed requires efficient motion and relaxation of the muscles, combined with correct performance. Increases in speed greatly increase the power of a karate technique. You also increase the strength of a blow by working your muscles in harmony, contracting them in the correct order without interference from opposing muscles. This coordination of the connections of the body results in maximum force at the moment of contact.

The major connections are at the shoulder, hip, and foot. Root your foot to the floor and actually grip the surface with your toes. Push your leg firmly into the hips. The action of driving the leg into the hip helps the hips to turn quickly. By keeping the trunk centered over the stance—not leaning too far forward or back—a strong connection is created between the trunk and the legs. As the hip turns, the trunk will also turn with the hips driving the arm forward. As the strike hits the target, tense both shoulders as if squeezing the armpit. This helps stabilize the muscles of the trunk on both sides of the body. With the shoulders equally tensed and not overextended, a strong connection is created between the shoulders and the trunk.

USING THE HIPS

In karate, the muscles of the seiken tandem (lower abdomen) contract to move the center of the body. This action, which provides the main source of power in karate technique, involves turning, twisting, or otherwise moving the hips. In karate, we often refer to "hitting with the hips." By breathing properly with the diaphragm when moving the hips, you can lower the center of your body to provide a stronger base. (In the West, we talk of feeling with the heart and thinking with the mind. The Eastern concept, however, is that the mental and spiritual [emotional] centers are located in the hara [the physical and spiritual center of the body] and that all power comes from that center.)

By twisting the hips, you bring the large muscles of the lower abdomen into the strike. As you twist your hips, keep them parallel to the floor, rotating quickly and smoothly on a level plane. Your upper body remains upright over the hips, turning in conjunction with the hip movements. That is, the hips, torso, and shoulders all turn at the same time. Remember to follow the rules of proper posture, head position, gaze direction, and so forth. You can twist the hips either in the direction of the strike or in the opposite direction. The term jun kaiten is used when the hips twist in the direction of the strike; when they turn in the opposite direction, the term is gyaku kaiten. The stronger and more common of the two movements is to twist the hips in the direction of the strike.

THE WITHDRAWING HAND

Karate uses reaction force. When striking, blocking, or thrusting, the opposite hand is pulled back sharply and quickly usually to the hip to balance the strike. This is called hiki-te (withdrawing hand). The quicker the pull backward, the faster the strike.

Strikes and withdrawals must balance each other. That is, straight-line techniques, like a punch or front kick, require a

Moving the hips. Block into a side-facing straight hanmi (left), then strongly twist the hips forward as you attack (below).

straight-line hiki-te; circular techniques, like a backfist strike or a roundhouse kick, require a circular hiki-te. Since high punches and middle punches travel in straight lines but at different angles, the withdrawal for each will be slightly different. When performing a low defend and turning to the side, the block travels downward to the side of the body in a circular movement. The fist of the withdrawing arm also moves in a circular fashion as a result of twisting the hip. Some very advanced practitioners can produce the same effect without withdrawing the hand, but the muscles in the shoulders, arms, and back must be trained to create this effect. Developing a strong, balanced withdrawing hand has one other important advantage: It requires that the muscles around the spine be bilaterally trained, thereby balancing the back and keeping the spine erect. This is important for stabilizing the body.

CHANGING STANCES

The center of gravity (the hip area) moves on a plane that is level with the floor. This allows the force of the blow, either an attack or defend, to travel the shortest and straightest distance to the target. To do this, bend the knees and ankles as necessary. When stepping, the moving leg naturally draws close to the driving leg and then slides lightly forward and out to the side for balance. This is considered a circular stepping movement. The driving leg propels the body, and thus the power of the technique, forward. Bend or straighten the knees and ankles as needed to move the hips level to the ground. Pivot on the heel, ball, or middle of the foot as appropriate. When you change stances or otherwise move about, perhaps while kicking, you may need to change from a left or right guard. Do this in such a manner that your arms come together, protecting the body from attack during the change. When attacking, move your weight forward; when defending, you can shift your weight backward. These actions provide dynamic stability and balance. For maximum effect, hold the technique back until the last instant, releasing this action just as the moving leg touches the floor. Firmly grip the floor with your foot at the moment of contact. Remember, you must properly coordinate your hand, foot, breath, and blow to achieve maximum striking force. As you practice, closely study how the hips move in stance changes, and combine this motion with attacking or defending.

STEPPING

There are two ways to step in karate. The action of driving off one leg and sliding the moving leg lightly forward is called fumi-dashi. One foot is driven in front of the other, and the stance changes. Yori-ashi means to slide the feet without changing the stance. This motion can be forward, sideways, or backward. One foot operates as the driving leg, providing the impetus for motion. The driving leg usually propels the opposite foot in the direction of the movement. With either method of moving or changing direction, pull your moving foot close to the driving foot. This provides for balanced movement. It also allows you to change the stepping method, driving foot, or direction of movement in mid-step if necessary.

BREATHING

Proper breathing is crucial to the success of a karate strike. There are a few breathing methods you can use to gain control of your breath.

• **Sei (tranquillity)**—One method to practice sei is to sit in a lotus position with your back straight and your hands palm up on your inner thighs. Begin by slowly and steadily inhaling through the nose. After so many seconds, quickly fill the rest of your lungs. Next, slowly and evenly exhale from the mouth for the same length of time you took to breathe in then quickly expel the remaining air. Use your diaphragm when inhaling; this will give you the feeling of filling your lower abdomen with air. When exhaling, try to place your tongue on the roof of your mouth and make a hissing sound. Making this sound will help you maintain a steady exhalation. It also has another use. As you listen to the sound of your breathing, this sound will have a calming effect on your mind and body, allowing you to forget the pressures of the day. Cleansing the mind enables you to concentrate totally on your practice. Sei can be used during mokuso to have a calming effect (see chapter 3).

• **Ibuki**—Ibuki breathing is a quick and forced exhale using the diaphragm and lower abdomen. The faster and more forceful the exhale, the quicker and stronger the blow. Since the muscles of the lower abdomen link the upper and lower connections, ibuki breathing becomes the primary factor in coordinating the body for power in a strike. Use this breathing method as you block and strike. Expel no more than 80 percent of the air in your lungs at any one time. This is the breathing method used to kiai (shout).

• **Nogare**—Nogare is a slow, forced exhale from the lower region of the body. As you breathe slowly, tense all of your muscles until they reach maximum contraction at the end of the exhale. Inhale as the body relaxes. This breathing technique trains the muscles of the body to flow together, tensing with the maximum possible force. Although nogare is primarily a training method, you can use this technique to tense your muscles strongly when needed, such as when breaking a grip.

• **Kiai**—Kiai is a loud, sharp exhale from the pit of the stomach that forces the muscles of the lower abdomen to tense sharply. Kiai provides tremendous strength and has three uses: to steel the body from a blow, to stimulate the muscles to a more forceful effort, and to break the attacker's concentration—that is, to destroy her ability to successfully conclude the attack. The kiai especially involves the diaphragm and the muscles of the lower abdomen. As an aid for using the correct muscles, make a sound like "hai" or "osu" (oos).

5

BLOCKS, FALLS, AND ROLLS

Blocks have many purposes in karate. You can use a block to begin an attack, to bring your opponent under control, to put your opponent off-balance, or to stop the attack before it begins. Blocks can redirect the attack and permit time for you to move to a more advantageous position. You can follow a block with a counterattack, or you can use the block itself as an attack. Blocks can be "soft," parrying a blow away from the body, or they can be "hard," stopping a strike at the point of origin or seriously damaging the attacker.

In using blocks, you must learn to make instantaneous decisions. What part of your body is your opponent targeting? What technique is being used? What is the attacker's intent? Which attack will be the primary strike? What action will the opponent follow with? Will there be an attempt to trap you with a series of attacks? You must be able to judge your adversary's intentions and choose the block that best controls the attack, that puts you in an advantageous position. It is usually better to block with the arm that will be closest to your opponent after you have shifted your body in response to the attack.

Each block only protects the edge of the body called the body defensive zone (see chapter 8). This provides maximum strength and closes the body to further attack. Once you have countered an attack, you do not need to continue defending against the attack. If you do not stop the block at the right time, the overextension of the block will cause a loss of leverage and open your body to further attack.

When performing the basic blocks, keep your hand in a fist position. This prepares the muscles on the blocking arm for the shock of contact and keeps your fingers out of the way. As you become more proficient, you can use other hand positions with the blocks. Practice blocking with both sides of the body and in various stances. A well-trained karate-ka can use a technique from any position and with either side of the body.

TECHNIQUE TIPS—BLOCKS

1. Time the block to the attack.
2. Twist your wrist strongly and quickly to add power to the block.
3. Execute the block in a way that puts you in a better position after the attack than before.
4. Time your blocks with the movement of your hips and breathing, and coordinate the block with the counterattack.
5. Move the blocking arm to a position of leverage that is not too close or too far from the body. This action is different for each block.
6. Keep the muscles in the body balanced and the spine straight. When blocking with one hand, withdraw the other hand to the side, ready to punch.
7. As you advance in rank, learn to balance the muscles on both sides of the body without withdrawing the opposite hand.

BASIC BLOCKS

Many people refer to blocks as *defends*. The four basic blocks found in every style of karate are the

- jodan-uke (upper block), which is used against an upper-level attack;
- soto-ude-uke (outside-inside block), which is effective against a face strike to a middle-level attack;
- uchi-ude-uke (inside-outside block), which is useful against a middle-level attack; and
- gedan barai-uke (downward block/downward sweeping block), which is used against a punch or kick to the lower part of the body.

Each of these blocks employs a quick twist of the wrist so that the forearm can strike against the incoming attack. For maximum leverage, you must position your elbows correctly at the end of each block. Each blocking arm must follow a smooth, coordinated path, with the movement of the elbow controlling the movement of the block. The elbow must follow a smooth, coordinated path from start to finish, ending correctly at the end of each block. The four basic blocks described on the following pages as a group involve the full range of movement of the shoulder.

UPPER BLOCK

For the jodan-uke (upper block), turn your fist palm side up, extend it across your stomach, then quickly raise your arm up above your head. Raise your elbow to the height of your ear, and place your forearm about a fist's distance above and forward of the top of your head. At the moment of impact, strongly twist your wrist outward and upward to about a 45-degree angle. When blocking, reach the other arm across the front of the body so that the elbows touch, protecting the solar plexus, then withdraw quickly to the hip. In this block, the blocking arm can collapse if you do not twist the forearm enough or if you twist it too far. This block is sometimes called a high defend or a rising block (age-uke).

MIDDLE OUTSIDE-INSIDE BLOCK

To perform the soto-ude-uke (middle outside-inside block), reach out with one hand to protect the front of the body and pull the other elbow behind and near the ear, with your fist palm side out. Strongly twist your wrist and circle the elbow forward and around to the middle of the body, the top of the fist just below eye level. At the same time, drop the elbow of your blocking arm to the middle of the chest in a position that allows the greatest leverage and withdraw the other hand strongly to the side. Center your blocking arm in the front of the body; when you are in a half-facing position, this will put the edge of the blocking arm at the opposite side of your body. This block is also referred to as an outside forearm block or defend.

MIDDLE INSIDE-OUTSIDE BLOCK

With the uchi-ude-uke (middle inside-outside block), bring the fist of your blocking arm, with the palm side of the fist facing downward, to the opposite hip. The other arm will touch at the elbow, protecting the solar plexus. Making sure the elbow does not rise, quickly twist the wrist of your blocking arm to rotate your fist upward to shoulder level as your other arm pulls strongly toward the hip. The elbow of the blocking arm is about a fist's distance away from the body at the height of the shoulder and the angle of the arm at the elbow is about 90 degrees. Block only to the side of the body. This is also referred to as simply a middle block or defend.

DOWNWARD BLOCK

To begin a gedan barai-uke (downward block), make a fist with the palm side facing inward. Extend your fist near the cheek and shoulder on the opposite side. Bring the other arm forward with its hand in a fist, palm side down. If possible, let the elbows touch, thereby protecting the solar plexus. Sweep the blocking arm downward and across the front of the body with the forearm twisting strongly at the point of impact. End the block with the fist a few inches above your leg. As you lower the blocking arm, quickly withdraw the other hand, palm side up in a fist, to the hip. Make sure you do not extend the blocking arm beyond the side of the body. This block is sometimes referred to as a low sweeping block or low defend. The Japanese word "barai" refers to sweeping.

OTHER BLOCKS

Karate employs many types of blocks that use both open and closed hands. Almost any movement of a body part can be a block, but certain actions are commonly used in karate. Many of the blocking actions are variations of those we have just studied, using the palm, wrist, back of hand, and so forth. Below are descriptions of some other common blocks.

SWORD-ARM AND KNIFE-HAND BLOCKS

Start the wanto-uke (sword-arm block) from a position near your opposite ear, using a knife-hand position (see chapter 6, p. 90), palm side toward the body. Move the block slightly downward and across the front of your body as the palm turns slightly outward with the wrist twist. In most styles of karate, the elbow is bent and the wrist straight. Some styles employ a shuto-uke (knife-hand block) that uses the knife edge of the hand instead of the forearm as the blocking weapon. In these styles, the arm is usually extended farther and the wrist is bent so that the fingers point upward. Another method is to bend the little finger side toward the wrist, sweeping across with the arm to hook an attack. The main difference between these two blocks is the blocking edge—either the forearm or the knife edge of the hand.

SUPPORTING BLOCK

The morote-uke (supporting block) uses the opposite arm to augment the strength of the block. An example of a morote-uke would be to put the palm of one hand on the other forearm as you prepare the block; doing this will help push the block into the target. As you strike the target, your supporting arm acts as a brace.

X-BLOCK

The juji-uke (X-block) is another two-handed block. Cross your arms and then thrust them together at the target. This block can be performed high or low or to either side. Many variations exist, and you can use the block with different hand positions. One way to use this technique is to block with one hand and strike with the other. Another way is to block with one arm and use the other arm to trap the attacking weapon.

DOUBLE BLOCKS

It is possible to use two blocks at the same time. A kakiwake-uke (wedge block), as its name implies, uses two blocks to separate a double attack. An example is to move both arms outward as in the knife-hand block but with the hands shaped into fists. Another example of double blocking is to combine a downward block with an outside-inside block. Carefully used, double blocks can be extremely effective.

SELF-DEFENSE TIPS

BLOCKS

This chapter covers three ways to do direct blocking: using a block as an attack or an attack as a block, using an attack as a simultaneous block and attack, and using the feet to block.

Using a Block as an Attack or an Attack as a Block

Frequently, you can use attacks as blocks just as you can use blocks as attacks. The difference is that you use a strike to hit the attacking weapon and a block to strike a target area. In competition it is frowned upon to attack a striking weapon, as doing so can disable that body part, injuring the opponent. On the street, however, this is an excellent ploy to use. An example is to trap a punch with one hand and use the other to block (strike) just above the outside of the opponent's elbow in order to dislocate the joint. Another example is to block strongly into the biceps, causing your adversary's arm to cramp.

Using an Attack as a Simultaneous Block and Attack

Often you will be able to use an attack to redirect the opponent's attack as you strike. A good example of this is to punch inside an attacker's punch, using your elbow to redirect his attack outward as you strike with your fist. This is an excellent and efficient technique for defense or competition.

If you punch inside your opponent's punch, you can use your forearm and elbow to block the punch and simultaneously strike back.

Using the elbow to block, strike your opponent in the same motion with a backfist.

Using the Feet to Block

The feet can also be used to block. For example, you can use a crescent kick to block a punch or front kick. A very effective technique is to use the feet to attack a connection (see chapter 4) as the opponent attacks. In this instance, the kick causes the opponent to lose equilibrium and thus lose the effectiveness of his attack. This technique is good for defense, but attacking the joints is not permitted in most competitions.

Kicking a connection will destroy your opponent's ability to continue the attack.

Using the foot to block a roundhouse kick is devastating.

FALLS AND ROLLS

Ukemi is the art of falling safely. Falling and rolling skills are not considered part of karate kihon; however many good karate schools include them in their curriculum. For many of us, the odds of falling are far greater than the odds of being attacked. Falling down stairs, slipping on ice, or falling off a bicycle are common occurrences that can cause serious injury. As for karate safety, most serious injuries happen to those who are not trained to fall correctly. All karate-ka should learn falling and rolling skills as part of their defensive techniques.

TECHNIQUE TIPS—FALLS AND ROLLS

1. Karate techniques work best when you are on your feet, so avoid falling whenever possible.
2. When falling, tuck your head forward or bend your head backward as needed so it does not hit the floor.
3. Point your toes up directly over the hips if falling backward or sideways. If you point them over your head you could fall on your head.

4. Do not slap too soon or at the wrong angle. Your arms could get caught under you, preventing the breakfall from working or injuring your arm or shoulder.

5. When slapping, do not strike the floor as in a karate strike, but slap the floor in a relaxed way.

6. When rolling, remember to do a shoulder roll rather than somersault forward or backward. A somersault is not well suited to recovering from a fall.

FALLING FORWARD

When falling forward, keep your head up and form a triangle with your arms so that the fingers touch in front of your face. The object is to break the fall by slapping the ground with your forearms and palms just before your body hits the ground. In this way, the impact is spread along the arms and hands. Some methods of falling require that you use your toes to hold the body off the ground as you make the slap.

FALLING BACKWARD

When falling backward, breakfall by slapping out to both sides with the forearms and hands, about 30 to 45 degrees to the side. This slap should take place the instant the body touches the ground and has the same purpose as the slap in falling forward. When slapping, start in front of the body. As you fall backward, tuck your chin into your chest so that your head does not hit the floor. Keep your toes pointing upward directly over the hips.

FALLING SIDEWAYS

When falling to the side, breakfall by slapping the arm and hand on that side 30 to 45 degrees out from the body at the instant your body touches the floor. Start the slap from the opposite side of the body. Be sure to tuck your head, chin on your chest, and to extend both legs out from the body and up from the hips; this is similar to falling backward.

ROLLING FORWARD

You will often be able to roll out of a throw. Depending on whether the opponent hangs on to you, either roll up to your feet or slap out as you do in breaking a fall. This is a particularly useful skill.

To roll forward, place one foot out front and form a circle with the arms, palms facing inward. Bend over and place the hand corresponding with the forward foot on the floor. Tuck your head inside the circle formed by your arms. Roll in a circle along the arms from the forward shoulder to the opposite hip and either slap the ground as in a breakfall, or continue rolling and come up standing. If you do this correctly, your head will not touch the ground. Be careful not to tuck one leg underneath the other as you roll, as this can cause injury. Some people who are skilled in falling learn to breakfall by beating the ground with their feet rather than slapping with their hands. This is useful if your hands cannot be used. Make sure you do not strike the ground with the feet; instead, slap with your feet as you do with the hand slap. A really

hard throw could cause you to actually roll over in the air. You could end that "roll" with a breakfall technique as described earlier. Knowing how to roll can help you control such a fall.

ROLLING BACKWARD

To learn how to roll backward, squat on the floor and start to roll backward. Reach over one or the other shoulder with your feet until they touch the ground. This will allow you to tuck your head so that it does not touch the ground as you finish rolling backward over that shoulder. Usually, you can regain your feet after such a roll.

CHAPTER

PUNCHES
AND STRIKES

In karate, you can use any part of the body as a natural weapon for attack and defense. The most common weapons are the hands and the feet. Elbows and knees also provide strong attacking weapons although they are not as versatile. When practicing these blows, it is normal to find that you have a strong and a weak side. Nonetheless, it is important to practice using both sides. Doing so will not only improve your action on both sides, it will prevent you from having weaknesses in your defense and offense.

Atemi means to strike the vital parts of the body. Not only must the proper part of the body be attacked, it must be struck with the right weapon in the right way. For example, a back-fist strike to the solar plexus will not have the same impact as a punch or front kick to this target. Additionally, the timing, distancing, and angle of the attack must be correct in order for atemi to have its maximum effect. The distance a strike can travel is set by the height of the stance. If a stance is high, the reach of the strike is quite limited. A lower stance will increase your extension range and provide greater stability, but it will also reduce your freedom of movement. This will reduce the options that you have available to attack and defend.

You will generally use four kinds of blows in karate. They are tsuki (thrusts or punches), uchi (strikes), ate (smashes with the knees and elbows), and keri (kicks). This chapter discusses the manner of execution, striking edge, and path to the target of the more common punches and strikes. Kicks and smashes are covered in chapter 7.

Punches and strikes are hand attacks. Punches thrust a part of the hand into the target, whereas strikes generally are whipped or arced into the target. Except for the spear hand, punches can attack any area of the body that is open to attack. Strikes are very useful in attacking the sides of the opponent, although the stronger technique is the punch.

PUNCHES

Many hand forms can be used for tsuki (punches). Most are variations using different parts of the hand as the striking weapon. Each hand position must be correctly formed to strike a target so that the hand is not injured and the force of the blow is fully applied.

TECHNIQUE TIPS—PUNCHES

1. Start in the proper kamae (upper-body position) and use the correct muscles in the correct order.
2. Coordinate the punch with the movement in the stance(s) and with breathing.
3. Keep the body relaxed until the moment of impact.
4. Concentrate on achieving instantaneous tension of all the body's muscles at the point of contact.
5. Most punches follow a straight line. Be sure the punch follows the shortest path to the target. To keep a punch traveling in a straight line, do not rotate the fist over too soon.
6. The quicker and more forceful the withdrawing hand (hiki-te), the faster and more powerful the thrust.
7. Keep unnecessary tension out of the shoulders, arms, and hands by not using unnecessary muscles.
8. Kiai at the moment of impact.

FOREFIST

Seiken (forefist) is not only the most popular of the hand positions, but probably is the strongest hand position used for punching. To make a strong fist, curl your first three fingers tightly into your palm, starting with the little finger. Then likewise curl the index finger. Lock your thumb down across the index and middle finger. The bones behind the foreknuckles of the index and middle fingers are the striking surface. Hold the wrist straight; be careful not to let it bend upward or downward and line these knuckles up with the supporting structures of the bones in the wrist and arm. By doing pushups on the foreknuckles, you will strengthen your wrists to support this powerful blow and also help to properly position the foreknuckles.

SPEAR HAND

A nukite (spear hand) is a hand form in which the tips of the fingers are the striking edge. You can use a nukite with all four fingers. When the index and middle fingers are used, it is called nihon nukite (two finger), and if only the index finger is used, it is called an ippon nukite (one finger). Nukite are best used against the softer, less muscled areas of your opponent's body. In forming the spear hand, extend your finger(s) outward; in the two- and four-finger variations, press your fingers against each other. Bend the thumb downward and press it against the index finger. Keep the wrist straight. You can strengthen your fingers by doing pushups on your fingertips.

A common way to use the spear hand is to bring the palm of the nonstriking hand under the elbow of the striking arm. This action can be used to protect or to block a strike downward with the spear hand striking over the block.

OTHER FIST POSITIONS FOR PUNCHES

Other fist positions are the ippon-ken (use of the middle knuckle of the index finger), nakadaka-ken (use of the middle knuckle of the middle finger), and hiraken (use of the middle knuckles of all four fingers to form a flat fist that serves as the striking weapon). In this latter position, your fingertips must press firmly against the top of the palm. In the former two positions, strengthen your index or middle knuckle by bracing it with your thumb.

Ippon-ken.

Nakadaka-ken.

Hiraken.

BASIC PUNCH

Start the sonoba-tsuki (basic punch) at the hip, with your hand in a fist, palm up, and your elbow pulled back. The other hand is generally out in front of the body, either in a guard position or in a completed blocking position. As you begin the punch, brush the elbows of both arms along the sides of your body as one arm pulls back and the other goes forward. As you extend the elbow of the punching arm past the front of your body, twist your wrist in a corkscrew fashion into the target, ending palm side down.

If you turn the fist over too soon, the elbow will flip away from the body, causing the punch to be weak. Take care to keep your shoulders level and the muscles of your chest and back firm; doing so will balance your muscle action and add speed and strength to the move. As you punch, quickly pull your opposite arm into a palm-up position near the other hip. The punch should target the centerline of the body.

You may see advanced practitioners begin a punch with the fist near the solar plexus, with the withdrawing hand simultaneously blocking. These shortcuts can work well but only if the muscles have been properly trained.

When using a punch, it is common to start the punch in the side-facing (hanmi) position of a front stance or cat stance or in a stance where the hips are side-facing to the target like a back stance. Then either twist the hips forward or step into a stance that allows the hips to twist into the target.

VARIATIONS OF THE BASIC PUNCH

Karate practitioners often use variations of the basic punch. An age-tsuki (rising punch) rises in a circular route to the opponent's nose or chin. A tate-tsuki (vertical punch) is a punch with the fist in a vertical plane and provides a strong body attack. A ura-tsuki ("close" punch) is similar to an upper jab. This method is useful when you are close to your opponent. A kagi-tsuki (hooking punch), strikes across the front of the body, with the elbow bent at a 90-degree angle. A mawashi-tsuki (roundhouse punch) swings in an arc toward the target, hitting with the thumb side of the fist downward. This can be used to strike behind your opponent when you are in close. U-punches involve simultaneous punches—one high and one low. The high punch is placed directly over the low punch. When the arms are held close together, this punch is called awase-tsuki (U-punch). When the arms are father apart, the punch is called yama-tsuki (wide U-punch or mountain strike).

REVERSE AND STRAIGHT PUNCHES

There are various ways to use a punch. The most common, and perhaps the most powerful, punch is the gyaku-tsuki (reverse punch). In a reverse punch, the striking hand is on the opposite side of the body from the forward foot. The power comes from twisting the hips, shifting the center of gravity, and driving from the rear leg. The reverse punch works best when the body moves in a smooth, coordinated fashion and is relaxed until the moment of impact. This technique is excellent for both countering strongly after a block or for launching a strong combination of techniques. The reverse punch is normally used from a side-facing (hanmi) position moving to a forward facing position or from a back stance to a forward facing front stance. Conversely, a choku-tsuki (straight punch) is a punch with the hand on the same side of the body as the forward foot.

Reverse punch.

Straight punch.

LUNGE PUNCH

Another common method is the oi-tsuki (lunge punch). Use the forward foot to strongly drive the rear foot forward and into a front stance while punching with the hand that corresponds to the forward foot. Throw the punch as your foot touches the floor. This method is often used for one-step sparring practice.

OTHER PUNCHING METHODS

Other types of punching include dan-tsuki (punching repeatedly with the same hand), morote-tsuki (punching simultaneously with both hands to different targets), and ren-tsuki (quickly punching two or three times by alternating the hands). Two more ways to punch are heiko-tsuki (parallel punch), which is two fists striking the same target at the same time, and hasami-tsuki (scissors punch), which is striking both sides of the opponent's body at the same time.

One way to use dan-tsuki is to grasp the opponent's guarding arm and force him backward, repeatedly punching over and under his arm. Ren-tsuki works well while advancing forward. The best way to use this is to reverse punch with each step forward. This is a very natural and effective way to attack. The two-handed punching works well in self-defense situations especially as someone is attempting to grab you or has grabbed you. While their hands are busy, you can use yours very effectively.

STRIKES

Uchi (strikes) is another classification of hand attacks. Strikes can vary depending on the path of the strike. A mawashi-uchi is an inside circular strike. It starts from an inside position opposite the striking arm and then travels out to the side of the striking arm. A soto mawashi-uchi (outside circular strike) starts on the same side as the striking weapon and travels inside toward the body. Tate-uchi are vertical or upward striking techniques. Yoko-uchi are strikes that travel sideways to the target. Most strikes either arc into the target or are whipped at the target. In many instances, blocks can be used as strikes and strikes as blocks; generally, however, blocks are closer to the body and use the forearm whereas strikes extend outward to the target and use a hand position.

Strikes are also defined by the hand position. The three most common strikes are the shuto-uchi (knife-hand strike), uraken (backfist strike), and kentsui or tettsui (hammer-fist strike).

TECHNIQUE TIPS—STRIKES

1. Coordinate the movements of the strike to the twisting of your hips and turning of your body.
2. Lead the strike with your elbow. If you can get your elbow inside the opponent's block, the strike will be unstoppable.
3. Twist your wrist or forearm in whichever way is appropriate to add power and speed to the strike.
4. Attack more quickly by not tensing your elbow or shoulder.
5. Relax your triceps after the strike, using your biceps to pull back your arm.
6. Extend your striking arm to its full length, but do not lock your elbow.
7. Do not confuse training methods with proper technique. While training, the striking arm is sometimes left extended; in proper technique, you must retract the strike.
8. Kiai as the strike hits the target.

KNIFE-HAND STRIKE

Shuto-uchi (knife-hand strike) is the popularly known karate strike. Bring the hand, palm side in, near the cheek and shoulder of the opposite side, then deliver it outward and slightly downward. Twist the forearm, strongly driving the knife edge of the hand into the target. To form the knife hand, extend the fingers straight out and touching. Force the palm side of the knuckles forward, arching the hand backward. Pull the thumb in and bend the top of the thumb downward. The knuckles between the fingers and the palm should be arranged so that you can squeeze the knuckles together without the hand collapsing. The meaty edge of the palm serves as the striking edge of the hand. This means that in a downward strike, the hand is at an angle to the target rather than vertical. As with most karate techniques, quickly and strongly draw the opposite hand, palm up, to your side. A variation of the shuto is to bring the striking hand, palm outward, near the ear on the same side, then strike from this position outward, twisting the palm inward toward the target. A shuto is a very strong strike. It is possible to knock an opponent out if the neck is properly struck.

Knife-hand strike, palm downward.

Knife-hand strike, palm upward.

BACKFIST STRIKE

A uraken (backfist strike) can be a vertical or horizontal strike. Basically, the back of the fist's foreknuckles serve as the striking surface. Use your shoulders, upper arm, and lower arm to whip out the fist in an arc-shaped path toward the target. To add power to the strike, twist the wrist right before contact. As soon as you make contact, quickly pull your fist back to where it started. Start this strike across the front of your chest with the palm side of the hand down, then whip it to the side. A variation is to start this strike behind the ear with your hand palm side outward and whip it downward. The backfist works best when striking parts of the face like the cheekbone, temple, or bridge of the nose.

HAMMER-FIST STRIKE

A kentsui or tettsui (hammer-fist strike) is delivered with the bottom (little-finger side) of the fist. This strike is similar to the backfist strike except the bottom of the fist is used as the striking surface instead of the back of the foreknuckles. A bottom fist is strong enough to attack most areas of the body.

OTHER HAND POSITIONS FOR STRIKES

Other parts of the hand are used to strike, and some strikes use part of the wrist or arm. A haishu (backhand strike) strikes with the knuckle area of the back of the hand. Strike the solar plexus, side of the head, or back of the opponent. A haito (ridge-hand strike) strikes with the inside ridge of the hand (opposite the striking edge of the shuto-uke). This is a good position to use to strike upward to the groin or around to the neck. Protect the thumb by drawing it to the front of the palm. In a teisho (palm-heel strike), the heel of the palm is thrust outward. Use it for striking the chin, nose, or solar plexus. Striking with the forward side of the palm is a seiryuto (ox-jaw strike). The face, collarbone, and sternum are good targets for this strike. To form a keito (chicken-wrist strike), bend the little-finger side of the hand downward. A bent-wrist strike is called a kakuto. As its name implies, you bend your wrist to strike the target. The chicken wrist and the kakuto work well as strikes to the arms, armpits, or side of the head. A powerful combination is to use the bent wrist or chicken wrist as a block and follow with a strike such as a palm-heel strike. The final two strikes are the kumade (bear-hand strike) and the washide (eagle-hand strike). For the bear hand, press the tips of your fingers against the edge of the palm and use the whole hand for striking. Use the bear hand to strike the eyes or ears. To form the eagle hand, press the tips of the fingers together, forming a semblance of an eagle beak. Use the eagle hand for striking soft areas of your opponent's body especially in the neck, throat, or behind the ear.

Backhand strike.

Ridge-hand strike.

Palm-heel strike.

Ox-jaw strike.

Chicken-wrist strike.

Bent-wrist strike.

Bear-hand strike.

Eagle-hand strike.

SELF-DEFENSE TIPS

STRIKES

Karate punches and strikes are some of the most powerful techniques a person can perform, making them very effective for self-defense. However, to be effective you must strike the correct target in the proper way. When striking a target, the angle of attack should be toward the center of the target. For example, a punch is very effective against the solar plexus, but when the opponent is facing sideways, the punch should be directed towards the lower rib cage. A knife-hand strike to the side of the neck should angle downward toward the trunk to obtain maximum striking force into the target. A hammer-fist strike can be very effective to the kidneys but not to the muscled areas of the abdomen, and an upward ridge-hand can effectively strike the groin. When striking the nose, use a downward backfist strike or a forward thrusting palm-heel strike.

A knife-hand strike to the neck can knock the attacker down.

A backfist strike to the bridge of the nose can stop even the most determined attacker.

CHAPTER

7

KICKS AND SMASHES

The best karate fighters are those who can use their hands and feet equally well. Kicks and smashes are a crucial element in both competition and self-defense. Kicks are attacks with the foot, whereas smashes involve the elbows and knees. Knee smashes are good for close-in fighting; fighters often substitute them for foot techniques when they are too close to kick. Similarly, they often use their elbows when the fighting becomes too close to use punches and strikes.

KICKS

There are many different ways to use the feet. Karate-ka concentrate on five main kicks, striving to use both legs equally well. These are the mae-geri (front kick), mawashi-geri (roundhouse kick), yoko-geri (side kick), ushiro-geri (back kick), and the mikazuki-geri (crescent kick). The kicking methods described in this chapter take a nonstylistic approach based on the methods used by major international competitors.

Kicks have some advantages over punches, strikes, and smashes. They can be more powerful and have a longer reach. However, because the body stands on one foot, excellent balance is required for kicks to be effective. Differences in hip structure also can affect kicking ability. Females have different hip structures then males and are usually more flexible for kicking.

Almost any part of the foot can be used as a kicking surface. Use the koshi (ball of the foot) for the front, roundhouse, and crescent kicks. Use the sokuto (outer edge of the heel) for the side kick and the kakato (heel) for most thrust kicks. Other parts of the foot that can be used as striking surfaces are the instep, tips of the toes, knuckles of the toes, and the back edge of the heel.

Kicks can be thrown from any stance and with either the forward or the rear foot. Use the forward foot to stop an attack and the rear foot to attack. Use a snapping action for a close opponent and a thrusting action for a retreating or farther away opponent. When kicking with the front foot, the weight must either be on or transferred to the rear leg. Stances in which the weight is on the rear leg, such as the cat stance, allow for easy kicking with the front foot. Conversely, when kicking with the rear foot, the weight must be either already on the front leg or transferred to the front leg. Most rear foot kicks take longer to execute because they have farther to travel to the target. However, their terminal velocity can be quite high, making the kicks very powerful.

Although high kicks look spectacular, kicks do not need to be high to be effective. High kicks are more a demonstration of flexibility than a show of superior technique. Middle- and lower-level kicks can be quite devastating. You do not need to learn to kick high, but you do need to train your legs in order to kick correctly. That way you can be effective whether your target is in close or requires extension of your limbs.

SNAP AND THRUST KICKS

Kicking methods can be divided between keage (snap) and kekomi (thrust). The choice between these kicking methods will depend in part on the kick you will use and in part on the distance to your target. Use a snap kick for a close opponent and a thrust kick for one who is farther away or retreating. Some kicks, such as the roundhouse kick and back kick, can be used only with either a snap or a thrust, whereas others, such as the front kick and side kick, can be performed either way. Snap kicks use a snapping action of the leg to propel the foot on an arc into the target. At higher skill levels, a springing action of the hips is also used by snapping the hips out and back with the kicking action. Snap kicks can be very quick. Use this action for front kicks, roundhouse kicks, and side kicks. Thrust kicks use the driving action of the hips to propel the foot straight into the target. They are more powerful than snap kicks and cover a greater distance. Use these for front kicks, side kicks, and back kicks.

BALANCE, STRENGTH, AND RETRACTION

In kicking, balance is important before, during, and after the kick. To help maintain balance, keep the kicking leg near the trunk of the body and the supporting leg slightly bent. During the kick, keep the foot of the leg on the floor pointed straight ahead (for front and crescent kicks) or toward the back (for roundhouse, side, and back kicks). This allows the hips to be thrust forward by the supporting leg. When pushing the hips forward, keep the upper body erect and the head directly over or in front of the standing foot. Do not lean backward, away from the kick. Doing so moves the weight in the opposite direction, making it easier for the shock of the kick to send you backward, losing balance and striking force. Grip the floor with your toes to strengthen your ankles and help maintain balance.

Strong kicks use the whole body. For snap kicks, use a spring action of the hips as described above. For thrust kicks, strongly push your hips into the kick with the standing leg, keeping the upper body erect. This drives the foot forward into the target. There is a shock when the kick hits the target. Keep the abdominal muscles tense as they provide the connection between upper and lower body absorbing the shock of the kick. Also straighten the standing leg as the hips move forward. This adds the strength of the standing leg to that of the kicking leg, which tremendously increases the power of the kick. After striking the target, quickly retract the foot to the starting position of the kick. This not only helps to maintain balance but prevents your leg from being caught, enabling you to kick again. If you learn to retract your leg quickly, your attacking speed will increase, adding power to the kick.

CHAMBERING

Chambering is the action of lifting the foot to the starting position prior to releasing a kick. Chambering is used in all but the crescent kick, which is delivered directly from the floor. To chamber, begin by bending your ankle and curling your toes upward, as if to touch the shinbone. The leg will point straight ahead with the foot directly underneath. At the same time, quickly raise the knee (not the foot) as high as possible, pulling the heel as close to the leg as you can. Keep the leg as close to your body as possible. For targeting purposes, lift the knee slightly higher than the imaginary line between the hip and target.

The chambering position for kicking.

TECHNIQUE TIPS—KICKS

1. Keep your upper body as erect as possible. Lean into the kick by pushing your hips in the direction of the kick.

2. Quickly retract the kick in order to maintain equilibrium and to be poised to kick again.

3. Straighten the standing leg to add distance, height, and power to the kick.

4. Keep your head over or in front of the standing leg, aiding balance and adding strength to the kick.

5. Chamber the foot with the toes curled up and ankle bent upward, knee high, and heel near the leg.

6. Always quickly retract your kicking leg. This prevents your opponent from grabbing it and enables you to kick again.

7. Learn to start a kick with the other foot as the first foot retracts. This enables you to kick again more quickly.

8. Kiai with the kick.

FRONT KICK

As the name implies, a mae-geri (front kick) is a kick directly forward of the body. It can be delivered with a strong snapping or thrusting action of the leg, sending the ball of the foot into the target. Keeping the supporting foot pointing forward, chamber the kicking leg as previously described. For either the snap or the thrust kick, point the toes of the standing foot forward and extend your leg one-half to two-thirds of its reach to make contact with the target. The best target areas for the front kick range from the lower abdomen to the solar plexus.

A front stance is a good stance to practice a snap kick. Pick up the knee and hold it in place, quickly snapping the leg out to the target and then back. Use the springing action of the hips to add power to the kick. As you kick, lock the ankle down and curl the toes up. This strengthens the foot and moves the toes safely out of the way so you can hit with the ball of the foot.

A thrust kick (shown on page 107) is best practiced moving forward out of a back stance. For the thrust kick, strongly push your hips forward with the standing leg. As the hips thrust forward, lock your ankle down and drop your knee slightly to drive the foot straight into the target. The triangle created by the hips, foot, and head shows the thrusting action of the hips. After extending the kick, quickly retract your leg to the starting position. A variation of this kick is to bend the ankle upward and thrust the heel into the target.

ROUNDHOUSE KICK

Use the mawashi-geri (roundhouse kick) to attack the side of your opponent, using a quick snap of the leg. It is effective for low, middle, or high targets, such as kicking your opponent's legs out from underneath him (not permitted in most competitions) and attacking the lower ribs, abdomen, solar plexus, or head and face. Although many karate-ka strike with the instep, the ball of the foot is more effective. The ball of the foot has a smaller striking surface, which concentrates the force of the blow and provides maximum power. One devastating modification of a roundhouse kick is to use the shin as the striking surface.

A good way to practice the roundhouse kick is to start in a back stance. Pick up your back leg and chamber your leg with the standing foot pointing forward. Continuing your motion, pivot on the standing leg so that the standing foot points as far backward as possible and align your shoulders, hip, and knee in a straight line. As you turn the foot, hips, and knee over, keep them on the same plane as the target. Combine the momentum of the pivot with a snapping action of the leg. Strike the target quickly, then retract the kick. To use your instep, point the toes out, with the ankle bent downward. To use the ball of your foot, keep the foot in the chambered position when you strike. You can straighten the standing leg to add height and distance to this kick. Be sure of your target, however, because you can easily lose your balance, especially if you miss. Sometimes when you are close, you can use the shin instead of the foot as the striking surface. This can be very damaging to your opponent.

SIDE KICK

A yoko-geri (side kick) is made with either the heel or the knife edge of the foot out to the side of your body. A side kick can be effective against almost any target because of its tremendous striking force. You can use either a thrust or a snap for the side kick.

A back stance is a good way to practice a side thrust kick (shown on page 111). To thrust a side kick, chamber the leg with the standing foot pointing forward. Continuing your momentum, pivot on the standing leg, pointing the standing foot as far back as possible. Align the hip joint and heel on a line to the target, keeping your knee in front of your solar plexus. Combine the momentum of the pivot with the thrust of the hips to drive the foot into the target. Retract the leg to the starting position, returning the body forward. When side kicking, the hips will roll over and face slightly downward, adding thrust to the kick. The kicking foot also will point slightly downward. Let your hips glide forward of the standing leg but keep the body erect and your head over or in front of the standing leg. When hitting with the heel, keep the toes curled up and the ankle bent upward. When hitting with the side edge of the foot, turn the foot inward so the outside edge leads the kick. For power, height, and distance, forcefully straighten the standing leg. When you turn the hips over, twist at the waist so that the chest and shoulders face in the direction of the kick. This allows you to easily recover in the direction of the kick. It also enables you to follow with a hand attack rather than expose your back to an attack.

To understand the side snap kick, start in a straddle-leg stance. Chamber the leg and snap the foot to the side without rolling the hips over or pivoting on the foot. Depending on the build of your hips, this can be very easy or very difficult. The more popular thrust kick can be performed by anyone and is more common in fighting.

BACK KICK

Perform a ushiro-geri (back kick) by turning backward and delivering a strong driving thrust with the heel. If you use a back stance, begin this kick by planting your pivot foot. Pivot backward and point it in the opposite direction of the kick in order to control the rotation movement. When turning backward, the order of movement is the head, shoulders, and hips. As you turn backward, chamber the kicking leg with the toes curled upward and the ankle bent up. Keep your heel as close to the leg as possible. The leg is in the rolled over position, aiming the heel and hips on a straight line to the target as you did in the side thrust kick. The difference is that now you turn backward instead of forward. Using the momentum of the backward turn, thrust the heel at the moment that your hips and heel are in line with the target. Retract your leg to the chambered position. You can then either step forward or continue pivoting back to the same stance you were in when you began to use the kick.

CRESCENT AND
REVERSE CRESCENT KICKS

A crescent kick (mikazuki-geri) is used to strike the face, abdomen, or groin. It is also an excellent technique to block strikes and kicks. In the description below, remember to keep the standing foot pointing straight ahead, or the technique will lose power and you will be in a vulnerable position.

Do not chamber prior to the crescent kick; instead, begin the kick from the floor. Swing your attacking leg out and upward and then across and down, striking at the center of your opponent's body. Curl the bottom of the foot inward, with the ankle bent up and toes curled up. Hit with the ball of the foot, then return the leg to the starting point of the kick. Crescent kicks can be used with spinning kicks (discussed on page 117). One variation of the crescent kick is the reverse crescent kick (gyaku mikazuki-geri). The reverse crescent kick swings in the opposite direction from the regular crescent kick—that is, inward and up and then across and down.

Crescent kick.

Reverse crescent kick.

JUMP KICKS

Any kick can be performed as a tobi-geri (jump kick).There are two ways to jump kick: Jump off the front leg and kick with the rear foot, or swing the rear leg out and up, quickly followed by a front foot kick. The leg swing usually serves to gain height or distance. If using a roundhouse kick, side kick, or back kick, first jump into the air and then twist the hips appropriately for the kick you are doing. Do not worry if you are not a good jumper. Jumping kicks are not the most important karate kicks. You can earn a black belt without being able to jump. Jump kicks, while spectacular, are good only for surprise. An alert fighter can easily move out of the way of a jump kick and counter successfully.

Jump side kick.

DOUBLE KICKS

A nidan-geri (double kick) involves two quick kicking actions with the same leg—for example, a front kick followed by a roundhouse kick. This skill requires good retraction of the foot in a kick. Double kicks can be very effective. The first kick is used as a fake, drawing the opponent's attention and block. The second kick takes advantage of the opportunity created, swiftly attacking the opening.

OTHER WAYS TO KICK

You can use various movements of your body with kicks. To execute a skip kick, take one skipping step, with your rear foot landing in the spot where your front foot started, kicking with the front foot. To catch a retreating opponent, you can hop forward on the standing leg to follow the retreat as you kick.

Spin and wheel kicks are excellent techniques for attacking the head or sweeping the feet out from underneath your opponent. For a spin kick, turn quickly backward and side kick or crescent kick as you turn. This kick requires that your weight be thrust forward. For a wheel kick, extend the kicking leg out behind you and then wheel the body around backward, turning the leg like the spoke of a wheel. Lift the kicking leg immediately, but do not release the kick until the last instant. Wheel kicks require good balance, with the weight centered in the hub.

For the spin and wheel kicks, plant your foot, pointing opposite the direction of the kick in order to control the rotational movement of the kick. In karate competitions, these two kicks do not always score because they cannot be thrown full force and pulled at the target. They can be excellent for self-defense, however, because they cannot be effectively blocked. The only way to avoid these kicks is to move out of the way.

Two other kicks commonly are used in karate. One is the hook kick. In this move, swing your leg around behind your opponent and hit by retracting the heel to the leg. The other is the ax kick. For this technique, swing a crescent kick up and then pull your heel down to the floor. This tactic is not permitted in most competitions.

SELF-DEFENSE TIPS

KICKS

Karate can be a very devastating means of self-defense if techniques are performed correctly. Kicking is most effective when the target is low. While a kick to the head can be devastating, the head is not an easy target to hit. Often flashy kicks are just that—flashy kicks. A front kick is a very strong kick and is excellent to the solar plexus and the lower abdomen. As far as kicking the groin, this target can stop both male and female attackers, but it is hard to hit with a front kick. Instead, strike the lower abdomen just above the public bone where the bladder is located. Side kicks and roundhouse kicks are excellent attacks to the knees and insteps. They also work exceptionally well to the lower rib area or solar plexus. Thrown correctly they can drive right through a block. Side kicks with the heel and roundhouse kicks with the ball of the foot can penetrate the ribbed areas of the chest and back. When in close, use the knees instead of the foot to strike with and target the groin, kidneys, and solar plexus. When using the knees combine elbow smashes to the chest and head.

When roundhouse kicking or side kicking, many fighters roll the leg over to its side as they bring up the knee to chamber. In many instances, kicking this way is effective, but it does allow your opponent to read your intentions before you chamber the leg. If you follow the general rules of chambering—ankle bent up, toes curled upward, foot underneath the leg, and heel pulled back to the leg—you do not commit to any particular kick. That way, you are able to respond to the actions of your opponent. Generally, if you were to kick with the right foot and your opponent moves to your left, the attack would most naturally become a roundhouse kick. Alternately, if the opponent moves to your right, a side kick would be best. If the opponent stays in front, you could use any of the three kicks. The key here is that your opponent cannot determine which kick you will use until the foot is actually launched, and you are reacting to the opponent, not him to your actions. This increases your options tremendously.

If the opponent moves backward as you begin to kick, you can simply perform a front kick.

If the opponent moves to the outside of your leg, follow with a side kick.

If the opponent moves to the inside of your leg, follow with a roundhouse kick.

SMASHES

Ate (smashes) are delivered with the knees and elbows. They are excellent for close-in fighting and can be devastating. They are legal in competition but difficult for the referee to see and judge. They are a natural means of self-defense because they are quite powerful and can be used effectively by a novice.

ELBOW SMASHES

An empi-ate (elbow smash) can be performed in many directions:

- Ushiro (backward)
- Otoshi (downward)
- Yoko (sideward)
- Mae (forward)
- Yoko mawashi (sideward roundhouse)
- Tate (upward)

Depending on the elbow smash, there are two parts of the elbow you can use for the strike: the forward, or forearm, edge and the point of the elbow. The backward, downward, and sideward elbow smashes use the point of the elbow. The forward, side roundhouse, and upward smashes use the forward edge of the elbow.

The methods of performing backward, downward, and sideward elbow smashes are very similar. For the backward elbow smash, extend your striking arm fully to the front, with palm side downward. Quickly rotate the forearm over as you strongly and quickly pull your elbow backward. For the downward elbow smash, reach the arm straight up, palm side outward. As you quickly pull your elbow down, rotate your forearm so that the palm side of your hand turns inward. To smash sideward, reach your arm across the front of your body. Quickly twist your forearm so your palm is up as you drive the elbow strongly out to the side.

The forward, side roundhouse, and upward elbow smashes start with the arm pulled back and the fist just above the hip, as in hiki-te (withdrawing hand). As the elbow drives out from the body, the forearm quickly twists downward, driving the elbow part of the lower arm into the target. For the forward and side roundhouse smashes, the hand turns palm-side down. The only difference between these two elbow smashes is that the elbow moves forward on the forward smash and across the front of the body on the side roundhouse smash. For the upward smash, rotate the forearm so that the palm faces the body as you raise the elbow. When doing an elbow smash, the hand is usually in a fist position, although a knife-hand position is sometimes used.

Backward elbow smash.

Downward elbow smash.

Sideward elbow smash.

Forward elbow smash.

Side roundhouse elbow smash.

Upward elbow smash.

KNEE SMASHES

A hiza-ate (knee smash) is a very powerful close-in strike delivered with the large muscles of the leg. It is extremely powerful and dangerous when used in-close to the opponent. Knee smashes are either tate (upward) or mawashi (roundhouse). For both knee smashes, you must quickly and strongly lift your leg. For the upward knee smash, simply lift the knee upward into the target. Move your hips forward to drive the strength of your standing leg into the strike. For the roundhouse knee smash, lift the knee quickly and pivot as you would in a roundhouse kick, striking with the knee. You will usually use a knee smash to replace a kick in situations where you want to strike with your legs but are too close to kick. When used correctly in-close, it is almost impossible for your opponent to see the smash coming and thus to block it.

Upward knee smash.

Roundhouse knee
smash.

TECHNIQUE TIPS—SMASHES

ELBOW SMASHES

1. Twist the forearm quickly to add speed and power to the strike.
2. Put your whole body behind the strike by strongly turning the hips.
3. Strengthen the forearm by using a fist or knife-hand position.
4. Do not use an elbow smash unless you are close to the target; otherwise, your opponent can avoid the strike.

KNEE SMASHES

1. As you raise your knee, prepare for the strongest hit by chambering your leg fully.
2. Use your standing leg to drive the knee smash into the target.
3. Only use the knee strike when you are close-in.

CHAPTER

8

STRATEGIES AND TACTICS

G ichin Funakoshi, considered the father of karate in Japan, said, "Karate ni sente nashi." ("There is no first attack in karate.") Without a first attack, there can be no offensive action. Without an offensive strike, there can be no defensive movement. This statement presents a problem. If there are no offensive or defensive actions in karate, why do we even consider such tactics? What he really meant is that both opponents exist as a complement. Each reacts in concert with the other, naturally flowing and evolving together, making a first attack an impossibility. Blocks are simply the counterpart to attacks, and attacks are the counterpart to blocks. This natural mergence with the opponent is called kawashi.

STRATEGIES

This chapter explains the strategies and tactics to use in competition. *Strategies* are general considerations for fighting. The first part of this chapter discusses the best way to take a fighting position, what is meant by taking the initiative, and the physical or mental moment to attack. The concept of defensive, escape, danger, and safety zones is presented, as well as the theory of closure. The second part of this chapter looks at *tactics*, more specific methods of attack and defense that you can use in competition, and at developing and testing these tactics. The ideas expressed in this chapter are not absolutes. My main goal is to give an approach toward designing your own strategies and tactics.

TAKING A FIGHTING STANCE

The choice of a fighting stance is a matter of individual preference. For example, the cat stance allows for quick movements to the side and would be good for a lithe person. A back stance, however, is good for defending against a strong attack but does not allow much mobility to the sides, making it the best choice for a sturdy person. A front stance is not a defensive stance, but moving into a front stance allows for a strong attack.

In many respects, it is the movements to and from the stances that are effective. Knowing this, most fighters use an intermediate position called a fighting stance. This is a position between a front stance and a back stance, providing a balance between power and mobility. Whatever stance is used for fighting, the stance should accomplish three things. First, it should allow you to protect your body from attack. Second, it should project an attitude of confidence and dominance. Third, it must allow you to respond quickly to any action of your opponent.

When taking a fighting stance, your hips should be side-facing and uncommitted. Center your weight on the balls of the feet to provide greater speed and flexibility of movement in any direction. Keep knees flexed, holding them closer together than you would in the front stance. In general, a higher stance indicates a kicker, a lower stance a puncher. Your stance should be neither too high nor too low. With proper training, you can learn to throw either hand or foot attacks from this position, making it hard for your opponent to read your intentions.

Do not unduly tense or relax your upper body. The preferred posture is side-facing, which reduces the forward target area. Most fighters bend the forward arm at the elbow, protecting the front of the body as in a middle guard (see chapter 4). Center the forward fist in the middle of your opponent's gaze. Bend your rear arm and cover the solar plexus. The line from your elbow to the fist should target the center of your opponent's body. Keep your head erect.

A fighting variation of the middle guard discussed below provides the best fighting posture. If you use a middle guard with the knees flexed, weight centered on the balls of the feet, and hips side-facing and uncommitted, you will have an excellent stance that can be used to both attack and defend. Most karate fighters use low guards when they are fatigued. Avoid a low guard unless you are lightning fast or your opponent is very tired. High guards leave the body too open to attack and tire the arms. It is more efficient to move from a middle guard to defend any part of the body against attack.

Fighting Guard. The most common fighting guard is similar to the middle-guard position. The main difference is that the hand forms are kept loose in the fighting guard and often both palms are up. Some fighters relax only their thumbs, keeping the other fingers clenched. Other fighters keep the hands open. These options allow more relaxation in the arms and shoulders for quicker movements. These ideas are not recommended for novices, as it is too easy to injure the hands without proper training and experience.

Free-fighting stance and guard.

Gaze. The gaze is important because sight is the primary source of information during a fight. Your gaze should take in the opponent in his entirety and not be lulled by his maneuvers. Keep your mind open, receptive, and otherwise uninvolved so that you can use your senses and properly discern the actions of your opponent. By focusing your eyes on one aspect of the opponent even for an instant, you lose your peripheral vision, and your brain will not be able to receive complete information. If your mind focuses on anything, you will either be unable to perceive, that is *translate,* the visual input or this translation will be slowed down. In either event, you will be unable to properly and timely analyze stimuli from your opponent and react quickly enough to prevent his dominance.

TAKING THE INITIATIVE

Well-trained karate-ka know when to attack and seize the initiative. There are three times when an opponent is vulnerable to a successful attack:

- When the opponent is thinking of attacking (*sen sen no sen*)
- When the opponent decides to attack (*sen no sen*)
- When the opponent actually begins the attack (*go no sen*)

Sen sen no sen is the ultimate goal of the fighter. This is the ability to suppress any desire on the part of an adversary to engage in a fight. This comes about through humble confidence and superior character. Sen no sen is the ability to take the initiative early by attacking at the moment the opponent's mind decides to attack and he is distracted by sending orders to the body. Go no sen is to take the initiative later, attacking at the point that the opponent's attack physically begins and beating the attack with your quicker reflexes. The moment of the attack is called okuri, and attacking at this instant is called deai-waza. This action takes both courage and skill. The greater your skill, however, the less the courage you will need.

THE MENTAL OR PHYSICAL MOMENT

No matter when you decide to attack, your attack will not be effective unless you take advantage of openings caused by your opponent's weaknesses and mistakes. Both mental and physical mistakes cause openings.

Physical mistakes include

- weaknesses in the guard,
- mistakes in attacks or defends, and
- failure to keep up with the pace of the fight.

You can cause your opponent to make physical mistakes by

- using continuous techniques that overpower or overload the ability of the opponent to defend,
- using blocks to break the opponent's concentration, then immediately attacking, and
- attacking when the opponent is at a disadvantage.

Mental mistakes include:

- making a wrong attack,
- misreading a feint and overreacting to it,
- letting your guard down because you think your opponent is also relaxing,
- becoming distracted or anticipating your opponent's actions, and
- worrying about your opponent's intentions.

Mental openings can be created by

- enticing the opponent to make an unfortunate attack,
- drawing the opponent's attention away through the use of a feint,
- causing the opponent to relax momentarily by letting him think you are not ready to attack,
- making the opponent's mind concern itself with unnecessary things by distraction or anticipation, and
- creating doubt or concern for safety.

Such tactics inhibit your opponent's ability to properly perceive stimuli and to react to your actions.

DEFENSIVE, ESCAPE, DANGER, AND SAFETY ZONES

The two attacks most commonly used in kumite (free-fighting) are direct, straight-in attacks and indirect, circular attacks. Direct, straight-in attacks include punches and front kicks. Indirect, circular techniques include roundhouse kicks and backfist strikes. The required angle of attack will vary with the intent and your choice of weapon and target. For example, if your opponent is in the corner of the ring, a direct attack, like a front kick or punch, will force her to try to escape to one side. Prevent her escape by immediately attacking again with an indirect strike, such as a roundhouse kick, to that side. If the opponent is near a boundary line (or an obstacle on the street), an indirect attack toward the line or obstacle would force him over the line or into the obstacle. An indirect attack to the other side, however, would allow him to escape.

There are four zones to consider during a fight:

1. The safety zone, where you do not need to be concerned with an immediate attack
2. The defensive zone, where defense or retaliation is necessary
3. The escape zone, where you may move to avoid an engagement or attack
4. The danger zone, where you are trapped and forced to engage without adequate preparation

The figure below shows where the defensive and escape zones are for both direct and indirect attacks.

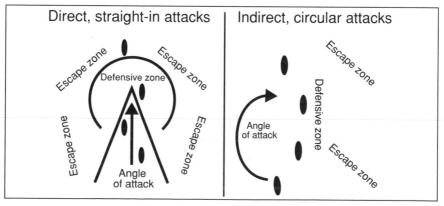

Defensive and escape zones.

You should be constantly aware of where the defensive, escape, and danger zones are as you move about. As a defender, seek to take the initiative by launching an attack from a comfortable place in the safety or defensive zone. As an attacker, attempt to put the defender at a disadvantage in her defensive zone. An alternative action is to attack in such a way that you will force her into the danger zone, thereby cutting off areas of escape and defense. This can force the defender into an impetuous movement. When attacking, use combinations designed to narrow the area in which the opponent can maneuver. As a defender, maneuver to prevent the opponent from closing you in.

The figures below illustrate these ideas. In the first figure, the opponent attacks with a front kick. The fighter responds by slipping to the side and blocking the leg. From this angle, the opponent is not

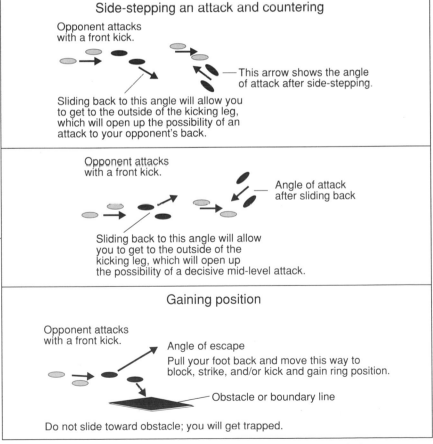

Defensive strategies—gaining the advantage. The solid black circles represent your beginning and ending position; the dotted circles your opponent's.

in a good position to defend. The second figure shows essentially the same concept but the defender moves to the opposite side requiring change in the forward foot. Finally in the last figure, the choice of tactics shown in the first two figures are affected by an obstacle, or in competition, a boundary line that creates a danger zone.

Defensive Sphere and Distancing. One way to understand the defensive zone is to use the example of a sphere. Imagine a sphere around your body that encompasses the reach of your arms and legs. This illustrates your defensive sphere. As long as your opponent's sphere does not intersect yours, you are safe. When the two spheres overlap, you must heighten your senses to prepare to attack or defend. Take a fighting position so that you can confidently attack, yet stay far enough away that you can easily escape your opponent's actions. Using distance in this way is called maai (distancing). The idea of maai is to be in a position from which you can attack or defend with only one step. This allows you to effectively move into and out of the opponent's defensive sphere.

Closure. The basic idea of closure is to move your body so that you can target the opponent with your weapons and be in range to attack, and yet maintain a position from which the opponent cannot retaliate. You achieve closure whenever you enter the opponent's defensive zone. When closing, try to maneuver so that the opponent loses the ability to use one or more of his arms or legs; this is called disconnecting the opponent's weapons. Learn to selectively disconnect the opponent's weapons as you move about. Then, when you are within range, you can attack with the most efficient weapons for the circumstances, knowing that the opponent will be unable to do likewise. As you work on this strategy, learn to move within range by using the best tactical weapon for the situation, not just your favorite weapons.

TACTICS

Tactics are specific methods of attack and defense. For example, a common tactic is to attack in threes. This means to attack consistently with three techniques each time. By shifting the timing of the techniques, you can easily cause the opponent to make a mistake, creating an opening for a successful attack.

Other common tactics are to break the opponent's balance, double kick, fake, press the opponent, and pattern your attacks.

Openings for attacks often occur at one of two points in a fight: at the start of an attack, when the opponent is concentrating on getting the attack off, or at the end of an attack, when the opponent is unable to continue the offense and must recover or change to defense. When cracks in the opponent's defense appear, you must immediately make a decisive counterattack, otherwise the initiative will be lost. To do this, you must plan out your tactics and practice them regularly.

When designing your tactics, select ones that are

- realistic for your abilities and level of development,
- learnable in the training time allotted, and
- built upon previously learned skills.

There are no absolute rules on kumite tactics. Any competitor can foil her opponent's well thought-out tactics if she has the speed, agility, and quickness of mind to read her opponent's intentions or to take advantage of her opponent's errors. Then again, some fighters just get lucky.

DEVELOPING TACTICS

In developing kumite tactics, there are four stages of practice fighting that are helpful in this area: kihon kumite, jiju ippon kumite, semi-free kumite, and jiju kumite. It is always best to practice fighting under supervision in the dojo.

Kihon Kumite. Kihon kumite is a form of practice in which the weapons, target, block, and counter are all prearranged. The number of attacks involved usually are one (ippon), three (sanbon), or five (gohan). The object of prearranged sparring is to become familiar with, and efficient at using, the basic karate techniques, stances, distances, targets, and movements. That is, you will learn how to perform the actions with good form and power and learn to turn techniques into smoothly flowing tactics. Practice is usually very formal, with partners beginning in a standing ready position. One partner takes a step back to indicate the attack is about to begin and then attacks on the command of the defender or instructor. After a time, attackers are allowed to attack at will.

Jiju Ippon Kumite. Once kihon kumite is mastered, the next step is to practice with jiju ippon kumite. The attacker's weapon and target is designated, but the defender often is allowed flexibility in the choice of blocks and counters. Distance is usually predetermined or within discretionary limits. This allows you to become experienced and automatic in the use of your tactics and to experiment and determine which tactics are best suited to your nature for the type of attack designated.

Semi-Free Kumite. This type of kumite permits the attacker and defender to move and attack at will. The weapons, target, counters, and blocks are all predetermined, but the timing of attack is not stipulated. This version of kumite allows a competitor to become skilled in judging distance, taking the initiative, shifting and dodging, breaking the opponent's balance, and taking advantage of chance and error. At the same time, the student gains in-depth knowledge of a specific tactic and how to use that tactic effectively in different circumstances and against different fighters. Usually practice starts with one attack and defend, but as the student advances, additional attacks and defends can be added.

Jiju Kumite. Jiju kumite (free-fighting) allows the participants, within reason, the free choice of weapons, attacks, and blocks. Free-fighting allows the use of protective and safety equipment and usually follows competition rules such as those of the World Karate Federation. This provides a controlled environment in which the student can practice all that has been learned. One way to perfect advanced tactics for free-fighting and to learn concentration and necessary fighting skills is to require the lower-ranking students to freely attack the higher-ranking students. Then the instructor limits the tactics of the higher-ranking students to those tactics that are desired to be reinforced. The lower-ranking students become versed in attack as the higher-ranking students learn how to deal with random action. Lower-ranking students should not worry about fighting higher-ranking students. Usually higher-ranking students are more skillful and experienced and will be safer sparring partners for lower-ranking students, helping to prevent injury. Higher-ranking students who take advantage of free-fighting with lower-ranking students are commonly disciplined.

BREAKING THE BALANCE

Kuzushi refers to upsetting the balance of an opponent. If you can catch the opponent's center of gravity outside the base of the stance, you can topple him over. There are three ways to do this:

1. **The leg sweep**—Sweep one or both of the opponent's legs out from underneath him.
2. **The takedown**—Force the opponent to lean over outside of the base of support, causing him to lose balance and topple over.
3. **The throw**—Rotate the upper and lower body about the middle by causing the opponent to fall over your hip, leg, or other body part.

It is not necessary to take the opponent completely to the ground to achieve a decisive technique. You can destroy your opponent's effectiveness just by breaking his balance.

For leg sweeps, catch your opponent's foot or leg just before she puts her weight on the ground. The best sweeps push the opponent's "heel through her toes." That is, push her heel toward her toes. Sweeps are often combined with throws and takedowns. Before a sweep, takedown, or throw can be effective, there must be an off-balancing. One way to do this is to strike on an angle to the weak direction of her stance before attempting the action.

Leg sweeps are dangerous, and you must perform them with caution. Never sweep, throw, or take down a person who has not been taught to fall correctly, as they could be seriously hurt. If you are sweeping a person who is standing on one leg, you could severely injure that person's knee, depending on your attack. Furthermore, it is easy to drop a person in such a way that your opponent can't perform a breakfall. This, too, can cause a serious injury. Always be careful how you sweep; hitting the opponent's foot or leg can injure your own foot, as well as harm your opponent's foot or leg.

Moving into position for a leg sweep.

Sweeping the foot up high.

Remember, karate competition does not condone injuring the opponent for the sake of gaining an advantage. Kicking your adversary's arms, legs, and joints is not permitted. Yet these tactics can be very effective street-fighting techniques because properly thrown kicks can literally knock the opponent off his feet as well as break his arms and legs, and dislocate his knee joints.

Double Kicking. When I was a fledgling black belt, I used to fight three or four times a day. One day, I realized three things: Bone-crunching blocks to the legs hurt, as does kicking someone's elbow or crashing shins together, and the more I fought, the more time I needed to heal. Then I had a revelation. If I threw a kick, and I could see that it would be blocked, it made sense to pull the kick back before the block hit or the kick struck an elbow or shin. This would save my shins from a painful experience. There was no need to complete the kick. I could just pull it back early and avoid the contact (and the pain), essentially making a very realistic fake. As I began doing this, I became aware of the openings created as my opponent tried to block the kick. So I began to follow with a second kick to the opening created by my first kick.

Later, I had two more insights. If I quickly withdrew one kick into a beginning position for another kick, I could save time getting off the second kick. If I were to bring up my other knee for a second kick as the first kick was being retracted, I could also save time in getting a second kick off with the other leg. These two maneuvers could cut 25 to 30 percent off the time necessary to kick twice, giving me a decided advantage over my opponents.

FAKING

Faking is used to draw the opponent's mind away from your intentions, forcing him to make a mistake that will give you an advantage. For instance, a strong fake strike to the head may open up the middle body if the opponent raises his arm to block the fake. Fakes may be as subtle as tilting the head, lowering the eyes, shifting the hips, setting the stance, or inviting an opponent to attack by an incorrect kamae. This creates an opportunity to take the initiative as your opponent, believing you are vulnerable, decides to begin or physically begins the attack. The main rule of faking is that the fake must be believable.

DOUBLE KICKING

Double and even triple kicking with the same foot is a very effective fighting maneuver that requires exact kicking skills. The idea is to make the opponent react to the first kick in order to create an opening for the second kick. For example, a hook kick to the head may cause the opponent to flinch backward, allowing a roundhouse kick with the same foot to catch him off balance. A strong front kick can cause the opponent to lower his guard. If you quickly retract the foot, you can shoot it over the top of the blocking arm with a roundhouse kick to the unguarded head. I have surprised many of my opponents by following a back kick with a roundhouse kick with the same foot. Most fighters retreat from a back kick and attempt to counter-punch as the kick passes. The roundhouse kick is an unexpected surprise because it requires you to change the direction of your pivot—something that most fighters cannot do.

There is a shortcut that makes double kicking work well: Start off with one kick and end with another. One example is the front kick—roundhouse kick combination. Pull the front kick back to the round-house position so you can execute the roundhouse kick sooner. Most fighters finish the front kick and then position for the roundhouse kick. By eliminating the unnecessary motion, you can attack sooner with the second kick. This presents an obvious advantage.

The opponent begins to block the first kick.

Quickly retract the foot.

Attack with a roundhouse kick over the top of the opponent's blocking arm.

PRESSURING AN OPPONENT

By keeping pressure on an opponent, you can learn a great deal about her fighting tactics or lack of them. Square off in a neutral position so that neither you nor your opponent invades the other's defensive space. As you later jockey back and forth, probing into the opponent's defensive space, the opponent will react. In this way, you get to observe her actions and reactions to your movements, enabling you to evaluate her fighting style, tactics, strengths, and weaknesses. This has the added advantage of occupying your opponent's mind with your movements. One fighting style that uses this tactic is sword-and-shield style fighting.

In sword-and-shield style fighting, fighters assume their guard by holding their forward arm out as if holding a shield and the back arm as if ready to thrust with a sword. The idea is that the forward arm (shield) protects the heart while the practitioner thrusts the sword forward. The clashing of the swords and shields presents an opening for the attack. If any part of the body can be caught outside the protection of the "shield," it can be successfully attacked. Therefore, the tactic is to move in and out of the opponent's defensive space protected by his "shield." By doing this, and by applying pressure to the edges of the opponent's defensive area, you can force his body into a vulnerable position. An alternative tactic is to force aside your opponent's imaginary shield. Either way exposes his body to attack. An added advantage of testing the sides of the opponent's defense is that you can increase the adversary's feeling of vulnerability. The opponent must constantly adjust position to prevent becoming exposed outside the protective area of his imaginary shield. By occupying his mind in this way, you can create a mental lapse, making it difficult for him to react to a preemptive attack.

PATTERN ATTACKS

When an opponent assumes a proper guard, the center of the body is protected. Karate fighters generally defend with arms or hands and rarely with legs or feet. If you can keep both of the opponent's arms busy, the only options that remain are for her to move out of the way or use a leg block. If you can move quickly enough, you can stop your opponent from moving out of the way. The general strategy is to fire off three techniques as simultaneously as possible in order to occupy the opponent's blocking tools and control where she moves. If these set-up attacks work correctly, the opponent will be in a precarious position to block any further attacks.

HIT-MOVE-HIT

Tai sabaki (body shifting or body waving) and kawashi (translated as dodging) are techniques for moving your body out of the way of an attack and then immediately counterattacking. Your goal is to avoid giving an opening while preparing to launch an immediate attack.

For example, when someone is stung by a bee, the natural reflex is to slap at that area of the body where the sting was felt. If you are struck by a punch or a kick, you would turn toward the source of the pain and attack in that direction. In the hit-move-hit technique, you would defend against a strike and then counterstrike your opponent (hit); you do not stay in the same place but instead shift your body away from where your opponent's counterstrike would be directed (move) into a position where you safely strike again (hit). You can continue this cycle of hit-move-hit for additional strikes.

Starting position.

As the opponent strikes forward with a punch, move the rear leg back to the side and block.

Immediately strike the opponent with a punch (hit).

After the strike continue moving to the side (move) and strike again (hit).

Finish by withdrawing out of range of the opponent.

Thus your goal is to keep your opponent's mind busy, his defenses spread out, and in a vulnerable position. This creates a weakness that can be exploited with the main attack. For example, draw the opponent's arms away from his center by attacking the outside areas. This opens his solar plexus to attack. Alternately attack to the center of the body and then attack toward the left side to draw his attention to that side. The primary attack, then, would be to the right side. Three attacks in rapid succession aimed at the same place can tie up the opponent's attention, enabling a swift attack to another target area to be successful. Do not use a pattern in such a way that the defense can easily flow from one attack to another, effectively nullifying your strategy. The farther you pull the blocking from the intended target, the more difficult it will be for your opponent to escape the final attack. Experiment until you find those tactics that work best for you. Do not, however, use them in a predictable manner so that the opponent can guess your intentions.

PATTERN ATTACKS

Many fighters attack in such a way as to keep the opponent's attention occupied so that when the real attack comes the opponent is unprepared to defend. One way to do this is to use a pattern of attacks that leads the opponent's mind and defenses away from the intended target. Once occupied, the opponent will be unable to defend your vital strike.

Quickly strike with a high punch, forcing a high block.

Immediately follow with a low punch, forcing a low block.

Without hesitating, attack high with a roundhouse kick.

After the first three attacks have spread out the opponent's defenses, quickly strike the unguarded middle with a reverse punch.

BREAKDOWN

There are four areas in which your fighting system can break down. First is an inability to move your stance. There are three possible causes of immobility: the failure to learn how to move correctly, fatigue, and superior tactics of your opponent. A combination of proper tactics, strength, and endurance training can help prevent this. Second, you might move in such a way that you disconnect your own weapons. Third, you might choose the wrong attack. Do not use just the attacks you feel comfortable with. Instead, learn the best attacks for each situation. Fourth, you might use incorrect tactics. For example, if you need a closure, attacking with an extended roundhouse kick would enable the opponent to easily negate the desired closure. You need to develop tactics to force a closure when you want one and to avoid a closure when you do not want one.

SELF-DEFENSE TIPS

CONTROLLING THE OPPONENT

Control in karate involves more than just being able to stop a full-force blow before it strikes the target. Control includes making your opponents respond in the way you want them to respond and to even make them think what you want them to think.

Karate is a defensive art. Therefore the art of control can be defined as putting yourself in a position of advantage to stop any potential or actual attack, while also putting your opponent in a position of disadvantage. Depending on the circumstances, this could include preventing a threatening situation from developing or avoiding one that has come up. Examples of this are not hanging around the wrong crowd or in the wrong place, and by ignoring an insult. If these tactics do not work and the situation escalates toward violence, then physical force may be needed in the form of escape or attack.

Escape is a defensive maneuver to get away from an attack. If escape is not possible, then attack is the last resort. Your attack must stop the opponent from continuing his attack. There is a very simple method of controlling a physical attack that allows you to move to a position of advantage, either escaping or attacking, depending on the circumstances and the need to escalate violence. Assume that someone is attacking you from the front with a grab, punch, or kick. Keeping one foot on the floor, step back to the side with the other foot and bring your arm across the front of your body. The motion of the attack will carry you forward, as though pushing open a door. Like that door, you swing open, using one foot as a "hinge" on which to pivot before the attack reaches you. Use the arm on the side of the "hinge" foot to block, guiding the attack(er) through the door. This will put you behind the opponent—a position of obvious advantage. Furthermore, all your weapons will be easily available, and your opponent will be in a difficult position to continue his attack. This is called tai sabaki (body shifting).

Starting position.

As the opponent attacks, step back and to the side with your foot as if you are a door pivoting on a hinge. This move quickly avoids the attack and puts you in a position of advantage.

Another way to escape an attack and control the opponent is to retract your forward foot to the rear foot while turning your body away from the attack and drawing the opponent forward. Then step out with your other foot to the side and attack. This is a method of kawashi (dodging).

CHAPTER

9

KATA

kata is a group of prearranged movements, in controlled patterns of exercise. Kata is designed to teach karate-ka the fundamental principles of attack and defense and to develop a better understanding and broader application of karate. Most karate schools require the mastery of kata as part of belt advancement. A high degree of discipline and control is required to perform kata, but these movements can be practiced by everyone: men, women, children, and the elderly. Many international kata champions are competing long after the kumite competitor's career ends.

Kata is an individualistic performance. Performing kata generates and stimulates creativity through the efforts necessary to correctly interpret the kata. Much like a ballet dancer who performs the movements unique to ballet with expression and meaning, kata is a vehicle of expression. In the performance of kata, a clear understanding of the kata and its expression and meaning is communicated.

Kata can be defined as a limitless study of a master's technique, training, and plan of attack. It is a statement of flexibility and an exercise of the mind, body, and spirit working together in concentration and awareness. Training in kata underscored the relationship to personal combat by including those concepts thought invaluable in the proper training of the fighter. The old karate masters, who were the fighters of their day, used kata as their major training method to formulate their thoughts, which they passed on to their successors. Thus kata became the textbook of combat training by the karate masters. Many of the skills and techniques that students learn in kata are those that are needed in actual combat: power, vigor, good form, breathing, zanshin (being relaxed and alert at the end of the fight), and so forth (see chapter 10). Kata, by eliminating the pressures of combat, allows for correct training of the physiological and psychological responses necessary for combat. These responses are difficult to practice in free-fighting.

Performing synchronized kata is a beautiful competitive event.

Essential to kumite training are upper-body positions, stances, and proper fixing of the gaze. Also important is zanshin, which means concentrated awareness, relaxed yet alert at the end of a battle. All of these can be studied from the various kata strategies. The student will require an understanding of the physiological movement, timing, and distancing. Ippon kumite that is kata-based facilitates the expansion and interpretation of the kata. Thus, combining the training of kata with the forms of kumite permits the correct understanding of technique. This allows the development necessary to combine the vital strike capacity with the ability to overcome a countermeasure.

VARIATIONS IN KATA

Every kata has its own value and character. Some kata are for group instruction, while others are philosophical statements. Certain kata exhibit strength and dignity, and strengthen sinew and muscle. Others are quick and flowing, requiring great agility. One style of kata uses natural patterns of movement, especially in the foot patterns, by virtue of a natural walking motion. Speed and proper timing are essential and the breathing is natural. In another style of kata, the feet step in a crescent-shaped pattern. Both systems of kata breathe with the movement, but in the latter, breath, while rhythmical, is forced (exaggerated) in accordance with each of the movements. A kata like Bassai Dai represents the use of contrast—composure and strength combine with agility and change. In addition, fast and slow movements combine with light and heavy application of strength. Direction changes are swift, expressing the feeling of turning disadvantage into advantage.

The beginning of the Bassai Dai kata.

Hangetsu (Seishan) kata, on the other hand, has a characteristic circular movement of the hands and feet for getting in close and off-balancing the enemy. Some of the techniques are fast and others are slow, but the hands move in coordination with breathing and with sliding the feet. Some styles of karate tend to specialize in one or the other style of kata. No system of kata is necessarily superior to any other. All will promote strength, technique, balance, rhythm, posture, and other assets that the student needs for karate. There are over 60 recognized kata today, and many variations exist among the different karate schools.

Weapons kata is similar to kata, except that the practitioners use ancient oriental weapons. The practitioners usually choose one of the following weapons:

- **Bo**—a staff about six feet long
- **Sai**—a short blunt sword with hooks above the handle
- **Kama**—a sickle with the blade curving out near the top of the handle
- **Eku**—an oar
- **Tonfa**—a baton-like weapon that has "side handles"
- **Nunchaku**—two pieces of wood connected by a rope or chain

These weapons are used as extensions of the hands and feet. Practitioners who are well trained in karate can easily learn to use these implements. Weapons kata studies correct use of the weapon and the strategies and interpretations involved with their use.

KATA AND RANK

In karate, the student can advance once she has a good grasp of the kata required for her rank. Kata requires timing, posture, balance, control, technique, and coordination. These skills determine the proficiency level of the karate student. At each kyu level, the student learns a new kata and reinforces her proficiency in the previous kata. It is not enough to just perform the movements in order without error. The student must repeatedly practice the kata until the kata becomes part of the expression of the karateka and she can use it automatically in a vital situation. The student can achieve this level only through persistent and earnest practice. Kata at the beginner's level generally mandates a specific method of performance. In more advanced kata, individual

Performing a weapons kata
with a bo.

expression is allowed, and the student may adjust the breathing
and rhythm patterns to her own technique.

KATA MOVEMENT

Kata movement can be divided into two types: basic and intermediate. The basic movements include postures, stances, blocks,
strikes, and kicks. The student will often perform these fundamental defensive and offensive movements in sets and in a specific
sequence.

Intermediate movements connect the basic movements. They
are fighting postures that link the paired sequences of defensive
and offensive movements and are responsible for beginning and
ending the kata at the correct place. These intermediate movements provide development of the mind and body. They usually
provide a break in the tempo and beat of a kata similar to a rest
in music. By affecting the rhythm, practitioners use these movements to express the meaning and principles of the kata.

PERFORMANCE POINTS

Competent performance of kata demands enthusiasm. The movements will be sometimes swift, sometimes slow, but always bold and powerful. In performing intermediate kata, the student must demonstrate proficiency in the following areas:

- Coordination of the hands, feet, eyes, and breath
- Awareness of the opponent
- Expression of the meaning of each movement
- Correct performance of the movements
- Maximum physical effort
- Proper balance of design and movement
- Stability of the center of gravity
- Proper breath control
- Proper gaze and focusing of the eyes
- Appropriate distribution of strength within the movements
- Internal consistency in the performance
- Balance
- Zanshin (remaining mind)

During the performance, the student should exhibit the psychophysical responses necessary to remove the kata from a purely rote performance into an artistic fighting mode.

The most important aspects of kata practice are noted below. The student must study these in relation to each kata.

- Each kata must begin and end on the embussen—the line of the kata movement. Many kata begin and end in the same spot.

- Each kata movement, as well as the entire kata, has its own meaning and characteristics.

- The nature of the technique—offensive or defensive, straight or hooking, and so forth—must be fully understood and expressed. Awareness of application and target is vital to express the meaning in the kata.

- The breathing methods change with the circumstances. It is important not to hold your breath. Basic karate technique has been to inhale on the block and exhale on the attack. Some styles, however, now call for the karate-ka to inhale just prior to each

Even young children can perfect karate kata.

technique and to exhale during the technique itself, whether it be a block or an attack. Kiai is also part of breathing, requiring a sharp exhale from the pit of the stomach. This contracts the abdomen, giving extra strength to a technique. A kiai also elicits the maximum psychological response of the performer.

• Each basic kata has its own internal rhythm. Gichen Funakoshi, considered to be the father of karate in Japan, had three cardinal rules of rhythm that lead the kata to zanshin. Mr. Funakoshi expressed these rules in his book *Karate-do Kyohan: The Master Text*. These rules call for the light and heavy application of strength (the correct application of power at the proper moment); the expansion and contraction of the body; and fast and slow fluent movements in technique. Once you fully understand the features of a kata and the exact meaning of each movement, you can correctly synchronize your degree of strength, speed of motion, and level of body flexibility to perfect the internal rhythm of the kata.

• Zanshin, which occurs at the end of a kata, is directly related to the correct rhythm pattern of the performance. Zanshin literally means *remaining mind*. It is the attitude or state of watchful waiting expressed at the end of a kata performance. It is the feeling of simultaneously extending the mind, body, and spirit to dominate the opponent; and exerting internal power forward, utterly cutting the opponent down.

TECHNIQUE TIPS—KATA

1. Start the kata relaxed, eliminating tension especially in the neck, knees, and shoulders.
2. Keep the center of gravity located in the hara.
3. As you practice the kata, imagine you are fighting an opponent and gaze in the direction of the attack and defense.
4. Practice until breath, stance, and movement are in perfect coordination, thereby increasing your speed and power.
5. Align the stroke of the technique along the proper path to the target and keep the muscles on both sides of the body balanced.
6. Correctly assume each stance and move smoothly on a straight and level path between stances. Do not bob up and down or weave from side to side.
7. Understand the rhythm and timing of the kata.
8. Express an exemplary attitude and spirit.

COMPETITION BASICS

Kata competition may look similar to ice-skating or gymnastic mat performances. The contestants perform combinations of movements, but there is a difference. Kata performance is not merely meant to impress judges and spectators through appearance. The karate practitioners must perform them according to correct understandings of principles inherent in each movement of the kata. Each movement in kata has a specific meaning or purpose unique to karate, as well as an associated strategy and application. These strategies and applications must be demonstrated by the competitor in the performance.

Individual and team divisions are included in kata competition. In many events, weapons kata is also included. Team competition is called synchronized kata. Team matches consist of competition among three-person teams performing kata in unison. Each team is entirely male or female.

Kata competition is preferably not held on mats, but on wooden floors. No specific size is required, but the area must be large enough to permit the correct performance of kata and the evaluation of the kata competition. Kata contestants are expected to wear a clean, white, unmarked gi—as is worn in kumite competition. For weapons competition, the participants must use weapons of authentic design, construction, and materials.

Performing a kata in competition.

INTERNATIONAL REQUIREMENTS

Although most karate competitions allow the performance of any karate kata, contestants in international competitions and team trials perform both compulsory (shitei) and free selection (tokui) kata. Compulsory kata were selected from the four major styles of karate that founded the WKF (see chapter 2). They represent a cross section of the major kata found in each of the four styles. Competitors may not vary the performance of these kata. By standardizing these kata, referees from different styles of karate can be cross trained to properly judge the performances. Free kata must be selected according to the schools of karate-do recognized in Japan; a list of these kata is published by the WKF. Here, too, no variations are permitted. The contestants must relate in advance the kata they will perform, and the name of the kata is entered on the kata score sheet. If the contestant performs a different kata, the referee will not score the performance.

The number of rounds for kata competition depends on the number of competitors. If there are more than 8 but less than 16 participants, two rounds of competition will be held. If more than 16 contestants take part, there will be three rounds of competition. The first round reduces the number of contestants to 16, and the second round, to 8. In these two preliminary rounds, only compulsory kata is permitted. Free selection kata is allowed only during the last round. Contestants may not repeat a kata except in certain tie-breaking circumstances.

SCORING

Kata normally is scored by a panel of five judges. One judge watches from each corner of the ring, and the chief judge sits at the head of the ring (see figure on page 161). A scorekeeper records the kata performed and the individual scores of each judge. An announcer calls the competitors in turn and announces the score given by each judge and the total score of the competitor. Each judge has two sets of cards that are used to visibly show his scoring of the kata. The cards are numbered 1 through 10, and 0 through 9. They are used to give a score between 0 and 10, using decimal points. Upon a signal by the chief judge, the judges hold up their scores. They are then read by the announcer and recorded by the scorekeeper.

At the beginning and end of each division in a tournament, all of the competitors and judges line up for a formal rei (bow). When called upon to perform, the contestant or team enters the competition area, bows at the ringside, and steps out to the line designated for starting the kata. After formally bowing to the referee panel, the contestant or team announces the name of the kata to be performed and then begins the performance. Upon completion of the kata, the contestant or team returns to the designated line and awaits the scores of the judges. In summing up the scores, the scorekeeper deletes the highest and lowest scores, and totals the final three scores, providing a final score. After the announcement of this score, the contestant bows once again to the judging panel and retreats from the competition area, bowing again at the ringside.

Criteria for Decision in Kata. In the kata performance, contestants are judged on their ability to demonstrate a clear under-

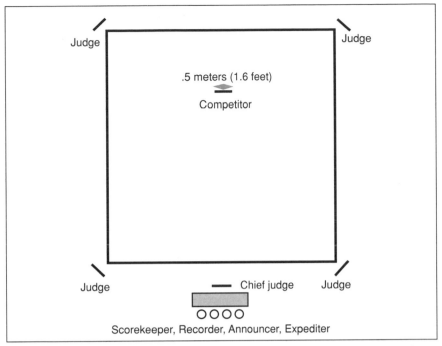

The positioning of the competitor, judges, timekeeper, scorekeeper, and other officials for the kata match. The .5-meter mark on the diagram indicates the mark where the competitor starts the performance.

standing of the principles of the kata and the special characteristic movements and postures. The competitor must proficiently perform these essential elements, as well as demonstrate good balance, correct focus of attention, proper posture, and other discerning features of the kata.

When determining the score, judges start at ten and then deduct for errors. The following criteria are used by the judges:

- For a momentary hesitation in the smooth performance of the kata, deduct 0.1.
- For a momentary but discernible pause, deduct 0.2 points.
- For momentary imbalance with barely a falter, deduct 0.1 to 0.3.
- For actual wavering in which there is a distinct but recoverable loss of balance, deduct 0.2 to 0.4.
- For a complete loss of balance or a fall, disqualify.
- For a distinct halt, disqualify.

In weapons kata, a contestant may be disqualified:

- if a weapon or the kata endangers or damages any person or property.
- if the contestant loses control of a weapon.

Determining the Winner. The competitor with the highest total score is the winner. Since divisions usually involve one round of competition, the score announced for each contestant is the score for the event. In the international divisions when there is usually more than one round, each succeeding round eliminates competitors, based on the score for that round. The score in the final round of the competition determines the winner.

If there is a tie, the scorekeeper will add the minimum rating of the three remaining scores back in for each tied competitor. If a tie persists, then the maximum rating of the three scores for each competitor is added. If the tie continues, the tying contestants must perform another kata of their choice. After the run-off, the judges will resolve any tie with a vote.

In breaking a preliminary tie in the international divisions, the contestant may not perform a kata he has already performed. The tie-breaking kata may be performed again in a later round but not as a tie-breaker. In the first preliminary two rounds, the tie-breaker kata must be chosen from a compulsory list. In the final round, the tie-breaking kata choice does not have to be on the compulsory list and can be any recognized kata (within the limits expressed here).

No karate training program is complete without kata practice. In addition to being a vital part of your progress from one belt to another, learning each kata helps the student develop attack and defense skills, as well as practice correct balance and movement. The performance points included in this chapter will help you focus on the most important qualities of the kata, whether you are interested in kata competition or just want to improve your kata practice in the dojo as a way to hone your fighting skills.

CHAPTER

10

KUMITE
COMPETITION

Kumite competition is held between two contestants, using free combinations of karate techniques. A score is awarded when an attack is targeted correctly, forcefully, and effectively. The competitors must control the force of their blows so that they do not injure their opponent. In kumite, the emphasis is not only to measure your physical strength against a competitor, but to raise the level of your mental, spiritual, and physical development. The winning contestant must not only show superior karate technique, but also spirit, self-control, and mental dominance over the opponent.

COMPETITION BASICS

Individual and team events are held at karate competitions. Team kumite matches consist exclusively of male or female teams, with three to seven persons per team. Individual competition is available for seniors, men, women, teens, and children of all ages. Single, double, and repechage elimination systems are used. Divisions are frequently broken up by age, experience, and rank. Adult competition frequently has weight classifications.

COMPETITION RING

The kumite match area is eight meters (about 26 feet) square and must be matted. Special kumite competition mats are available today and are used at all the important competitions. Boundaries are measured from the outside edge of the markings, so the boundary line is considered in bounds. There is also a warning zone 1 meter (3.3 feet) inside the boundary line, which helps the competi-

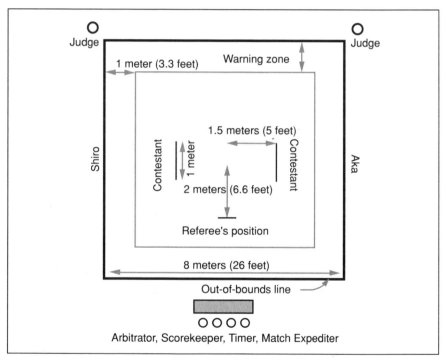

The layout of the kumite ring. The ring is 8 meters square with a warning line 1 meter from the outside of the ring. The judges sit in chairs at the corners of the ring furthest from the referee. The referee stands 2 meters back from the center of the ring with his back to the arbitrator, scorekeeper, timer, and match expediter, who sit at a table outside the ring. At the start or restart of the match, each contestant stands on a 1-meter long mark 1.5 meters from the center of the ring. Shiro (white) is on the left of the referee and aka (red) is on the right.

tors know when they are nearing the out-of-bounds area (see below).

Uniform and Equipment

Competitors must wear a clean, white, unmarked karate-gi. The sleeves of the gi must be at least half way down the forearms but may be no longer than the bend of the wrists. The trousers must be long enough to cover at least two-thirds of the shin; neither the sleeves nor the pants may be rolled up. The jacket, when tightened around the waist with the obi, must cover the hips but may not extend farther than mid-thigh. Women may wear a white T-shirt under the jacket. Headbands are not allowed. Competitors must have clean, short fingernails and may not wear metal or other potentially harmful objects, such as rings, hair slides, or hair grips. Glasses are forbidden, but soft contact lenses can be worn at the contestant's risk.

Most competitions require the participants to use safety devices. These devices are defined as equipment necessary to prevent injury to the competitors. Such gear usually consists of approved hand mitts, mouth-guards, and groin-guards. In international divisions, soft shin pads are allowed, but shin/instep protectors are forbidden. Women may be allowed to wear additional protective equipment approved by the WKF, such as breast protectors. Any use of bandages or braces because of injury must be approved by the referee council on the advice of the official doctor.

In junior and other noninternational divisions, additional protective equipment is often permitted at the discretion of the tournament director. This can include headgear, shin/instep protectors, and arm pads. There is some concern that blows to the head while wearing headgear can cause more serious trauma to the brain stem than blows taken without the headgear. Thus, while many events require head protectors, others do not. Those that do not permit headgear use a matted ring to protect the fighters should they fall. The uncontrolled use of protective equipment could encourage competitors to fight with less regard for the safety of the opponent because the protective equipment reduces the possibility of being injured themselves. The object of safety equipment is to prevent injury, not to encourage harder hitting.

Competitor in fighting uniform.
Notice the hand guards and mouthpiece.

OFFICIALS

Kumite is judged by a shushin (referee), one or more fukushin (judges), and a kansa (arbitrator). There are also charters, score-keepers, match expediters, and two timekeepers (one for the match time and one for injury countdowns). Besides the match officials, there is a chief referee; for major events, there is a control commission. The chief referee assigns the control commission, assigns the referees and judges, and decides matters not covered in the rules by consulting with the match officials. The control commission usually directs the immediate activities at the ring but does not have any impact on any specific match. Some large tournaments may assign a ring director to each ring; the ring director assists the chief referee in his duties and coordinates and controls the competition at a ring.

The main judging system used in international competition is the two-flag, or split-mirror, system. The referee conducts the match, awards all penalties and scores, announces the outcome of the match, and controls the area around the competition ring. He moves about the mat area of the ring, shadowing the fighters. (Common referee commands are shown in table 10.1.) The judges,

TABLE 10.1
Common Referee Commands

Ai-uchi	Simultaneous scoring. No point awarded for either contestant's technique. Referee brings fists together in front of his chest.
"Aka (shiro) ippon."	"Red (white) scores ippon." Referee obliquely raises his arm on the side of the competitor scoring, palm forward.
"Aka (shiro) no kachi."	"Red (white) wins." Referee obliquely raises his arm on whichever side the winner is standing, palm forward.
"Aka (shiro) waza-ari."	"Red (white) scores waza-ari." Referee extends his arm downward to the side of the competitor scoring, palm forward.
Atenai yoni	Warning without a penalty. Referee turns toward the offending competitor and raises one hand in a fist, with the other hand covering it at chest level. For any other penalty, the referee turns toward the offending competitor and crosses both hands at his chest.
"Atoshi baraku."	"A little more time left." The timekeeper gives a signal 30 seconds before the end of the match. Referee announces "atoshi baraku" to the competitors as they move about the ring.
Hansoku	Foul. The referee points his index finger to the face of the offender, then announces the other competitor as the winner. After indicating such a penalty, he awards no kachi (winner) to the opponent.
Hansoku chui	Warning with an ippon penalty. Referee points his index finger to the abdomen of the offender. After indicating such a penalty, he awards an ippon to the opponent.
Hantei	Judgment. Referee announces "hantei" and consults with judges to arrive at a decision.
Hikiwake	Draw. Referee crosses his arms over his chest, then extends his arms out to the sides, palms facing forward.
Jogai	Exit from fighting area. Referee points his index finger to the competitor and then to the out-of-bounds line. He then awards a keikoku, hansoku chui, or hansoku, if warranted, to the offender and grants the appropriate score to the other competitor.

(continued)

TABLE 10.1
(continued)

Keikoku	Warning with waza-ari penalty. Referee points his index finger to the feet of the offender. After indicating such a penalty, he awards a waza-ari to the opponent.
Kiken	Forfeit. Used for a renunciation, to renounce or quit the match, or a bye. The referee points toward the contestant's feet. Immediately after announcing kiken, the referee awards the match to the other competitor.
"Moto no ichi."	"Original position." Referee orders contestants back to their original positions.
Mubobi	Warning for lack of regard for one's own safety. Referee bends his arm at a 60-degree angle and points with the index finger to the side where the offender is standing. Referee then awards a keikoku, hansoku chui, or hansoku, if warranted, and grants the appropriate score to the other competitor.
Shikkaku	Disqualification. Referee points his index finger to the face of the offender and then points away from the competition area, signaling the competitor to leave the area.
"Shobu sanbon, hajime."	"Three-point match, begin." Referee stands on his line. No hand signal is made. After the announcement, the referee steps back and to the side so the arbitrator can see.
Shugo	Judge called. Referee beckons with one arm to the judge to come over for a discussion.
Torimasen	Unacceptable. Referee crosses his arms, then extends them to each side, palms facing backward.
"Tzus-ukete, hajime."	"Resume fighting, begin." Referee stands on his line, then steps back into a front stance. He points one hand toward each competitor and then brings the palms of his hands toward each other. Next, he steps to the side so that the arbitrator can observe the action.
"Yame."	"Stop." Used to interrupt or end the match. Referee chops downward with his hand as he moves forward. The timekeeper stops the clock. ("Jikan" is sometimes used as the command to end a match, signaling that time is up.)

who sit in the two corners of the ring opposite the referee, advise the referee by signaling their opinions with flags. The role of the judges is not, however, to judge the performances—only to provide information to the referee. The referee uses that information to make the correct decision. The role of the referee is very strong under this system; the judges have a lesser role due to their limited vision of the match. The arbitrator supervises the match and ensures that the rules are followed. He is also responsible for the charting, scorekeeping, and timekeeping functions for a particular match. The arbitrator does not express an opinion in the judgment of the match.

CONDUCTING THE MATCH

The duration of a kumite match is normally two or three minutes of fighting time. Competitors attempt to score ippon (the equivalent of one point) and waza-ari (the equivalent of a half-point). All kumite matches are sanbon shobu (three-ippon matches). The competitor to first score sanbon or who is ahead at the end of the match is the winner. When the score is tied at the end of a match, the referee calls for a hantei (vote for a decision). The referee and judges vote on whether to award the match to one or the other competitor, or to declare a hikiwake (draw). If a vote declares a draw, an encho-sen (sudden death) is fought. If the match is still tied at the end of the sudden death, the referee calls again for a vote, and the referee and judges must choose a winner.

BEGINNING THE MATCH

At the beginning and end of each competitive division, the competitors and officials line up for a formal bow. In international competition, a formal bow also takes place at the start and end of each match. In some events, the fighters bow to each other when they enter the ring. At the start of the match, the contestants stand at the edge of their respective sides of the ring. The competitor who is designated aka (red) wears a red belt and stands at the right side of the referee. The other competitor, designated shiro (white), wears a white belt and stands at the left side of the referee. The referee then calls the contestants to their starting lines. At the same time, the referee and judges go to their positions. The match is in play when the referee announces, "Shobu sanbon, hajime!" ("Three ippon match, begin!") At this command, the referee steps back from the line, signaling the competitors to begin fighting.

The start of a kumite match.

HALTING THE MATCH

Kumite matches are usually stopped by the referee in the following situations:

- When a scoring technique or a penalty occurs
- When a jogai (out of bounds) occurs
- When a contestant breaks the rules of the match
- When a contestant is injured or shows signs of an illness or other problem
- When a contestant grabs his opponent and does not perform an immediate effective technique
- When one or both contestants fall or are thrown and no effective techniques follow
- When there is confusion in the match
- When time runs out

When halting the match, the referee will call "Yame!" and signal by slashing his hand down and stepping toward the competitors.

Injuries and Accidents. Injuries and accidents cannot be fully avoided in kumite competition. No matter how closely a competitor tries to follow the rules, mistakes can happen. The rules stipulate which actions are to be taken by the referee if there is an injury or accident in competition. If an injury or accident results in a contestant being unable to continue the match, the winner is chosen according to the following guidelines.

A kiken (forfeiture) occurs when a contestant refuses to continue, abandons the match, or is withdrawn at the direction of the referee. The grounds for abandonment may include injury not ascribable to the opponent's actions. When two contestants injure each other at the same time or are suffering from the effects of previously incurred injuries, and the tournament doctor declares both of them unable to continue, the match is awarded to the fighter who is ahead in points at the time. If the score is equal, a hantei is required to decide the outcome of the match. If a contestant injures his opponent in such a way as to cause the opponent to be withdrawn from the match, the injured opponent will win through the foul or disqualification given to the participant who caused the injury. If a contestant withdraws because a previously existing injury was aggravated, this would not necessarily result in a foul or disqualification against the opponent.

Any contestant who wins a match due to having been injured by his opponent cannot fight again in the competition without permission from the doctor. Should that competitor be injured in a second match and again win due to his opponent's foul, the competitor will be immediately withdrawn from further kumite competition at that tournament. The contestant's name will go forward on the chart for the next round, and he will lose that round by forfeit.

Ten-Second Rule. In order to prevent fighters from faking injury to gain an advantage, any contestant who falls, is thrown, or knocked down and does not fully regain standing within 10 seconds is considered unfit to continue the match and will be automatically withdrawn. Time is kept by a timekeeper, and a warning bell sounds at seven seconds; the final bell follows at ten seconds. Depending on intent, fault, or accident, a forfeit, loss of match, or disqualification may be given to the harming party.

ENDING THE MATCH

The match is over when time runs out or when one of the contestants earns a score of sanbon. When time runs out, a bell is sounded. This bell signals the end of the scoring possibilities in a match, even though the referee may not halt the match immediately. To end the match, the referee calls "Yame!" and the contestants return to their original positions. The referee will verify the score. If the match has been won, the referee announces the winning contestant. If the score is tied, the referee conducts a vote. To do this, the referee calls on the judges for their opinions, and a decision is sought. The officials can declare a winner or a tie.

RULES AND SCORING

We would like to think that when the referee raises his hand to announce "No kachi" ("winner") that the victor is recognized without a doubt as the better fighter in the match. At international competitions we would like to think that when the gold medal is awarded, this winner is the most feared fighter in the world. Is the winner the best fighter in karate competition? Not necessarily! Referees are told that the most *correct* fighter must win. This is not necessarily the best fighter. The winner is the best fighter as defined by the rules of the competition.

Just like baseball, in which runs are scored, and soccer, in which goals are scored, karate competitors score ippon and waza-ari. Often these concepts are referred to as points or half-points, but this is incorrect. The concepts of ippon and waza-ari are more than just points or half-points. Just to hit the opponent before she hits you is not enough. Karate is not a game of tag. It is not that you hit, but how you hit. Therein lies the difference between a mere point or half-point and an ippon or waza-ari.

The rules used most often for karate kumite competition are those of the World Karate Federation (WKF). Over 150 countries, which are the members of the WKF, use these regulations. An understanding of these rules is vital to anyone who competes in karate competition. The regulations are designed to elicit a certain type and standard of technique. For example, certain techniques, such as wheel kicks, cannot demonstrate kime (controlled power, see p. 174) and are therefore not easily recognized for points under the rules. Thus, the rules have an inherent bias in their application. It makes no sense to prepare for any type of karate competition with techniques that will not be recognized under the rule system in effect for that competition. In order to succeed in competition, the karate competitor must understand what he is trying to accomplish. To do this, he must know and understand the rules of the competition he has entered.

The actions that the rules recognize and encourage affect the way a match is fought. This includes the competitors' techniques and tactics, strategies, and measures of range and distance. Permitted target areas also affect the type of techniques and tactics used. For example, to forbid the groin as a target area permits different distancing and ranging tactics than would be the case if the groin were an acceptable target. In order for an aspiring fighter to excel, he must train with the idea of ippon in mind and discard peripheral techniques that will not be ippon. To do this, the fighter must repeatedly practice ippon tactics and techniques.

This chapter generally relates to the WKF rules for elite international competition, but the underlying concepts are the same for other levels of competition. The standards for technique are appropriately reduced for youth and below-black-belt divisions, but all aspects of the requirements for ippon must nonetheless be demonstrated.

SCORING BASICS

To receive an award of ippon or waza-ari, the competitor must inflict a powerful karate technique to a legal target area while the match time is in play and the competitor is in bounds. (The opponent may be out of bounds.) In awarding a score, the referee first identifies the scoring contestant as "aka" (the fighter wearing a red belt) or "shiro" (white belt). He then announces the scoring area attacked (middle or high), the general classification of scoring technique used (punch, strike, or kick), and the score awarded (waza-ari or ippon). When a penalty is awarded, the announcer identifies the fighter being penalized, the level of penalty, and the award to the other contestant.

Being awarded an ippon.

Kime. Kime is the explosive use of power in karate. It requires the total focusing of the body, mind, and spirit at the instant of contact. The fighter focuses not only on the energy of the karate blow but also on the effect that the strike is intended to achieve. For kime to be at its strongest, hara (the physical and spiritual center of the body) and weapon must be unified in concentrated awareness. If any of these factors do not act in concert, kime will not be present.

Target Areas. The target areas consist of the head, face, neck, chest, abdomen, and back. The face is generally considered to extend to one centimeter above the eyebrows. The shoulders are not a scoring area, but the shoulder blades are considered part of the back. The abdomen is not limited by the belt, but extends to the pubic bone. The front of the neck that includes the windpipe, carotid arteries, and jugular veins is a target area, but the referee will penalize any contact to the throat unless the victim brought the contact upon himself.

In Bounds. Jogai is the name of the penalty for stepping out of bounds. A contestant cannot score when out of bounds; however, a competitor who is in bounds can score on an opponent who is out of bounds if the action takes place before the call to stop. Not only will the score be awarded, but also the out-of-bounds penalty. The lines that show the boundaries of the ring are considered to be in bounds. If any part of the attacking competitor's foot is over this line, the referee will issue a penalty.

Match in Play. Scoring can occur only while the match is in play—that is, between the announcement to begin (hajime) and the signal to stop (yame). A fighter cannot earn a score after time is called, but can get a penalty for failure to follow the referee's instructions. The only exception comes at the end of the match. The time's-up signal determines the end of scoring possibilities, not the call of yame.

Other Considerations. Ai-uchi (mutual scoring) is a situation where opponents land simultaneous scoring techniques. This is rare, and neither contestant receives a score.

A competitor may grab the opponent, but an effective scoring technique must follow quickly. If one or both of the competitors fall, the fighting can continue. There is little scoring potential from a prone position, however, and the referee will break up the action to prevent injury.

Pointless circling and other movements that waste time or avoid combat are against the rules. The referee expects the competitors to initially test each other but, within a short time, the fighters must deliver deliberate and effective attacks and counterattacks. If this does not happen after a reasonable interval, the referee will stop the match and caution the offender(s). Constant retreating is penalized. (Be careful to avoid retreating, especially during the closing seconds of a match.) An effective technique is valid if the fighter delivers it at the same time that the referee signals the end of the match. A competitor cannot score after the order to stop, and may even be penalized for persevering.

CRITERIA FOR IPPON

There are six specific criteria for ippon, and all must be present to score. If a technique is not acceptable for ippon, a waza-ari may be given. While two waza-ari are combined in the total score to account for one ippon, a waza-ari is not one-half an ippon. A fighter receives a waza-ari only when the technique is almost equal to an ippon. If any one criterion is completely missing, the competitor receives no score.

The six criteria for ippon are good form, correct attitude, vigorous application, correct distance, proper timing, and zanshin (remaining mind).

Good Form. Good form means that the kihon (technique) is correct. Proper technique depends in part on the style of karate the fighters use, but generally includes matters such as not bending the wrist when punching, keeping both shoulders down and the spine straight, not overextending the technique, and making sure the body remains coordinated and strong.

Correct Attitude. In order to score, the competitor must demonstrate the correct attitude. To do this, he must control the opponent and set up a situation to score or take advantage of the opponent's mistake. The officials must see that the technique is meant to score. Ippon or waza-ari are not granted for accidental strikes. If an attack is made with a flurry of techniques and one happens to land, the scoring requirements would not have been met. One way to bring an official's attention to the technique is to kiai as the vital strike is delivered.

Vigorous Application. Vigorous application requires that the competitor execute techniques with vitality and power. Power includes speed and strength. If a fighter executes actions without vitality, he cannot score.

Correct Distance. Correct distance (maai) and proper timing go hand in hand. Correct distance means that the attacker could extend the strike into the target. Not only does this involve the extension of the hands and feet, but also the competitor's ability to extend the hara (physical and spiritual center of the body) into the attack. If the body cannot get behind the technique, the distance to the opponent is too close. If the competitor fully extends the body and weapon, he can receive no score even if the technique impacts the target area.

Proper Timing. Proper timing means that the attack hits the target at an angle that could cause damage. The rotation of the opponent's body to and from the attacking weapon is important, as is the direction in which the opponent is moving. In the case of a retreating opponent, the attacker must move farther and faster than the opponent in order for the technique to have an effect. In that situation, the officials must decide whether the blow, if taken to completion, could have caused more damage. If not, there is no score. This is often seen in the case of a kick that hits and then pushes out against the opponent. The push will deny any possibility of getting an award. The opposite situation must also be considered: To avoid an opponent's attack, the competitor must either block the attack or move away farther and faster than the attacker.

Zanshin. Zanshin (remaining mind) is the state of continued commitment that "remains" after the blow has landed. The contestant with zanshin maintains total concentration and awareness of the opponent's potential to counterattack and expresses this through maintaining an impenetrable posture. Posture, however, is only the physical expression of the mental state. Zanshin is a heightened alertness of the mind to the matter at hand. Concentration must not end until dominance is assured. In the kumite match, this dominance occurs when the referee recognizes your technique by calling a halt to the match.

Technical Exceptions. There are five technical exceptions— that is, techniques that may be awarded an ippon even if they are of waza-ari quality. These exceptions require a waza-ari to be elevated to an ippon level. According to current WKF rule interpretation, these exceptions are either scored as ippon or are not scored at all. These technical exceptions are

- high kicking to the head or face,
- scoring at the precise moment the opponent attacks,
- deflecting an attack and scoring to the unguarded back of the opponent,
- sweeping or throwing, followed by a scoring technique, and
- delivering more than one blow in succession, with all blows scoring and no interruption by the opponent.

High kicks are more likely to score ippon.

PROHIBITED BEHAVIOR

Karate, like other sports, has its own system of penalties for actions that violate the regulations. Karate is a sport of skill and control, and its rules have been designed to strongly discourage injurious behavior for the purpose of gaining an advantage. The referee uses penalties to control the pace of the match and to prevent injuries. If a competitor breaks the rules, the referee may grant an award to the opponent or even give him the victory. This decision will depend on the nature and circumstances of the action.

The five penalties used in karate competition, in order of severity, are listed below.

- Atenai yoni—unofficial warning. The opponent receives no added score.
- Keikoku—a waza-ari penalty. The opponent receives waza-ari.
- Hansoku chui—an ippon penalty. The opponent receives ippon.
- Hansoku—loss of the match. The opponent's score is raised to sanbon.
- Shikkaku—disqualification. The referee removes the competitor from the competition.

Shikkaku is a penalty for disturbing behavior. The punishment may extend beyond disqualification, possibly resulting in additional penalties, including expulsion or suspension.

Penalty System. Each category of penalty escalates independently of the other categories. The penalties for jogai (out of bounds) and mubobi (failure to raise a defense) start at a warning and escalate at each succeeding occurrence to keikoku, hansoku chui, and hansoku (see table 10.1). Contact and control penalties, however, need not start at a warning. Each infraction is penalized based on intent, fault, and seriousness of the injury, if any. Once a competitor receives a penalty for a contact or control infraction, the next penalty must be greater than the prior penalty award even if the following infraction is less serious. A contestant who receives a hansoku chui for hitting his opponent too hard will get a hansoku for the next infraction, even if it is only slight.

Contact Penalties. Contact penalties include

- attacks to the groin, joints, or instep;
- attacks to the face with open-hand techniques;
- contact to the throat area;
- dangerous throws that make it difficult to fall safely;
- techniques that, by their nature, are not controllable;
- repeated direct attacks to arms or legs;
- movements that waste time; and
- purposeless grabbing, wrestling, or pushing.

An attacker will receive a penalty if contact was excessive or if he causes the opponent to suffer an injury. The referee will determine the degree of penalty based on whether the strike was accidental or deliberate, and the seriousness of the injury, if any. Remember that a second instance of a contact or control penalty will escalate upward. If the opponent who was struck failed to raise a defense or was at fault, a mubobi could be given, as discussed below.

Control Penalties. If the competitor does not control techniques to any target area, a penalty for excessive contact or lack of control can result. Control to the head, face, and neck must be absolute. Control to other scoring areas must be reasonable. In the case of kicking techniques to the head, there is a greater tolerance for contact with the target, but the fighter must control the kicks and not cause injury. In many national and local competitions, any touch to the head, face, or neck is considered an error in technique and will result in a penalty. Any technique that strikes the throat will be penalized unless the hit is caused by the recipient.

Out of Bounds. Jogai (out of bounds) occurs when a competitor escapes from the match. Since the boundary lines are considered in bounds, a competitor is out of bounds whenever all or a portion of any part of the body touches the floor outside the boundary line. A participant may step out of bounds and not receive a penalty if she earns an award just before exiting the match area, or if she is pushed or hit and falls out of bounds. Participants are penalized only if they attempt to escape from the match area to avoid competition.

Lack of Regard for Personal Safety. Mubobi is a contestant's lack of regard for his own safety. This is the failure to take a defensive attitude to protect oneself. Mubobi was instituted at world-level competition to reduce occurrences of faking injury for the purpose of gaining an advantage. An example would be a situation in which the contestant launches a committed attack without adequate preparation for defense. Such an attack is without regard for personal safety. Should the competitor be hit, the opponent may not be at fault. Fairness requires that the referee give a penalty to the offending fighter.

Disqualification. Referees give shikkaku (disqualification) for serious disregard of the rules of competition. Disqualification can be directly imposed, without warnings of any kind, and can lead to the strongest of censures, up to and including suspension for life. Circumstances for disqualification include

- acts that harm the prestige and honor of karate-do, such as showing disrespect, swearing, rude gestures, and poor sportsmanship;
- disobeying the referee's orders;
- becoming overexcited and jeopardizing the flow of the match;
- acting in a manner that is dangerous;
- returning to the contest area without the doctor's consent; and
- deliberately violating the rules of the tournament.

Feigning an injury is a serious infraction of the rules that can result in disqualification. Exaggerating an injury that does exist is less serious and may result in a penalty. Discourteous behavior toward the competitor or toward the officials is also grounds for disqualification. This is true even if the contestant is not the one who displayed the rudeness. That is, the participant can be disqualified even if his coach or other members of the contestant's delegation behave in such a way as to harm the prestige and honor of karate-do. Malicious behavior, regardless of whether actual physical injury was caused, is also grounds for disqualification.

The referee must define the extent of the disqualification. He may disqualify the offender from that division, from the whole tournament, or even for life. The referee will make a public announcement of disqualification. Any competitor who receives a disqualification may appeal and is entitled to a hearing. He may be reinstated at any time following proper procedure.

REFEREE CONSIDERATIONS

Since you now understand what a score is, let's take a look at what the referee considers while he observes a strike.

When a strike occurs, the referee must simultaneously determine a number of factors:

- Was the strike the result of a karate technique?
- Was the strike properly targeted?
- Was the quality of the strike good enough for a score?
- Did the strike contact the target?
- Was the strike sufficiently controlled?
- Was the striking competitor in bounds?
- Was the match in play?

If the answers to all the above are yes, then the competitor will receive a score. If the strike lacked control, the referee will consider the target hit, then consider the following questions:

- Was the contact excessive for the target?
- Was there an injury?
- Was the degree of injury major or minor?

- Was either contestant at fault?
- Was the hit accidental, deliberate, or malicious, or was it a mubobi?

Depending on the decision of the officials, anything from the award of an ippon, to loss of match, to a disqualification can occur on any strike.

Attacking at the precise moment of the opponent's attack is very skillful and is awarded ippon.

PREPARING FOR COMPETITION

Karate competitions take place virtually every weekend, but only a few major events are held each year. This section discusses how to prepare for a special event by using a seasonal plan. This plan considers the off-season, preseason, in-season, and peak season as being four different training periods.

Off-season starts three to four months prior to the competition. Work on muscle strength, general conditioning, and flexibility. Learn new karate skills and refine previously learned skills. Use prearranged one-step sparring to study timing and distance and to remove errors in techniques. This is when you should attain your fighting weight, which needs to be maintained throughout the season.

As you approach the preseason period, six to eight weeks before the event, begin to refine your skills and techniques into tactics for use in competition. Increase the intensity of your training. Simulate competition through the use of semi-free kumite 30 to 40 days before the first competition, begin in-season training by practicing your techniques under or near competitive conditions. For this, use as many partners as possible. Increase the intensity of semi-free kumite, simulating competition to eliminate any deficiencies in tactics. Use competition drills and regular competition to test tactics, sharpen your skills, and focus your mind.

The last few weeks before the event is the peak season. Concentrate on improving your speed. Practice under competitive conditions at full intensity. Taper off about seven days before the main event to allow your body to heal and rest.

Right before the competition, get a few nights of good sleep. Eat a healthy sport diet of 60 percent carbohydrates, 25 percent fat, and 15 percent protein. Keep yourself well-hydrated. The day of competition, eat a good meal, and take steps to maintain your fluid and energy levels throughout the competition by replacing lost fluids and energy.

During this seasonal training period, relax mentally. Meditation is good for this. Your mind must not dwell on worries or concerns, as this interferes with one's mental state for competition. During the event, you will need to forget about mistakes and concentrate on what is happening at that instant. In fighting for your life, the only important thing is what is going to happen right now! You must maintain this attitude for you to do your best.

Finally, not all events use exactly the same regulations. Before you compete at any event, get a copy of the rules to prepare yourself for that particular competition.

Whether you are preparing for karate competition yourself or are more interested in simply watching competitors to learn more about correct techniques and solid tactics, knowing the rules of kumite competition will help you be ready for your performance by eliminating any surprises or distractions and by allowing you to follow the action without confusion. As you get ready for competition, make the only unknown factor be your opponent. Learn the rules and procedures of kumite competition and prepare yourself both mentally and physically using the seasonal tips I discussed previously so you'll be at your peak and ready for the fight.

CHAPTER

11

CONDITIONING

Having started karate training, do you wonder what you can do between classes to enhance your abilities? Basic physical and physiological fitness can complement your training. Karate conditioning can improve flexibility, strength, speed, and endurance. Flexibility increases your range of motion, while strength improves power and endurance and tunes the body to burn energy efficiently. This chapter will discuss flexibility and look at the use of free weights and variable-resistance machines. I will explain the uses of plyometric exercises and speed training. I will also cover cardiovascular fitness for karate, as well as interval and circuit training. Finally, the chapter will explain the use of a heavy bag and a punching board to help you develop awesome striking force. If you use the specific karate conditioning described in this chapter, and if you correctly design and follow your conditioning workout, your body will be ready for the challenge of karate competition at any level. In addition, you will be in great shape and capable of defending yourself.

FLEXIBILITY

Most karate warm-ups include ten to twelve exercises that directly relate to your flexibility needs. First warm up, then use flexibility exercises to reduce the chance of injury during the workout and to eliminate sore muscles afterward. One way to decide which stretching exercises are best is to note which muscles are sore after karate practice. Those are the muscles that would benefit most from flexibility exercises. You should also include stretches in the cool-down period. Because the body is warmed up at that time, some believe that athletes derive a greater value from stretching during the cooldown than the warmup.

There are three common methods of stretching. One is the static stretch, in which you slowly stretch and then hold for 8 to 10 seconds. The second is the contract/relax stretch. After stretching out for 8 to 10 seconds, briefly contract the muscle and then stretch again for 8 to 10 seconds. You can easily do static stretches by yourself; many of the contract/relax stretches work best with a partner. The third method, ballistic stretching, is no longer recommended. Bouncing as you stretch can easily overextend the muscles and result in injury. Ballistic stretching can have value, but only experienced athletes who are familiar with this method should use it.

A sample karate flexibility exercise program includes the following exercises:

- **Head roll**—Bend your neck, then slowly roll your head a few times in each direction.

- **Arm swings**—Swing your arms back and forth, clapping your hands in front at shoulder level and in back of your body as high as you can for about 8-10 seconds.

- **Shoulder rotations**—Swing your arms a few times in a big circle, first toward the ceiling and then toward the floor.

- **Trunk twists**—Keep your hips straight while you twist a few times at the waist in each direction. A variation is to spread your feet, lean over, and form your hands into fists. As you twist back and forth at the waist, touch the floor on the outside of each foot with the knuckles of the opposite hand. Do this for 8-10 seconds.

- **Back stretch**—This is a four-part exercise. Start with your feet shoulder-width apart. Touch the floor with your hands, then reach back between your legs; draw up and then lean back. Return to the beginning position. Repeat this exercise 8-12 times.

- **Front leg raises**—With your toes curled up, swing each leg straight upward in front of the body 8-10 times.

Front leg raise.

Side leg raise.

- **Side leg raises**—Swing each leg up into a side-kick position and then back down, repeating 10-12 times.

- **Straddle stretch—** Take a front stance, then bend the front knee and drop your weight down as low as possible. A variation is to drop the back knee by setting the back leg on the ball of the foot. Hold this position for 8-10 seconds.

Straddle stretch.

- **Toe touches—**Sit on the floor, legs straight out in front, and touch your toes. Hold this position for 8-10 seconds.
- **Peacock stretch—**Squat over one leg and put the other, toes up, out to the side. Press the extended leg to the floor, holding this position for 8-10 seconds.

Peacock stretch.

- **Seated V-stretch**—Sit on the floor, legs straight, with your feet as far apart as possible, and then slowly stretch forward and hold for 8-10 seconds.

Seated V-stretch.

- **Quad stretch**—Kneel on the floor, hands on the heels, then push your hips up and lean backward, again holding this position for 8-10 seconds.

Quad stretch.

STRENGTH TRAINING

Muscular fitness for karate involves the entire body. The training varies, however, with the roles of the various body parts. Develop your lower body, including the knees and ankles, to provide a strong base for endurance and power. Strengthen your arms, legs, and shoulders to absorb the shock of blocking without losing speed. Your trunk becomes strong to endure physical punishment, yet remains flexible to provide smooth coordination and balance between the arms and legs. Speed and power are increased by stronger muscles, and with the right exercises, strength training can also increase neuromuscular skill. A strength-training program using free weights or variable-resistance machines can accomplish these goals.

WEIGHT AND REPETITIONS

To receive the greatest benefits from strength training, do the exercises in three to five sets of 8 to 10 repetitions each. If you do the maximum number of repetitions, you should perform the exercises at 66 percent or more of maximal resistance. Older individuals may find that they need as many as five to eight sets to develop maximum strength. To figure out how much weight to use, determine the maximum amount you can lift for each exercise. This is called the one-repetition maximum. Reduce this weight until you can perform just three sets of 8 to 10 repetitions. This weight should be around 75 percent to 80 percent of the one-repetition maximum (from a table describing maximum lift based on repetitions developed by Mike Clark, Strength and Conditioning Specialist, University of Oregon).

If you are unaccustomed to weight training, you may want to start light and increase the weight until you can perform three sets of 8 to 10 repetitions. Over time, you should increase the weight. One method is to start with a weight you can lift for one set of 10 reps. Then increase the weight each set and lower the number of repetitions. Strive to perform ten reps for all sets, then increase the starting weight and begin again.

STRENGTH-TRAINING PROGRAMS

Just about any strength exercise can build up the body for karate practice, but certain exercises are more valuable for this purpose than others. Following are two sample muscular training programs. These programs include the major muscles, as well as special exercises specific to karate needs. One program uses free weights; the other employs variable-resistance and isokinetic machines, which are available at most health and fitness centers.

Of the two programs, variable-resistance training is more beneficial for developing strength and your entire range of motion. It is also safer for speed training. Free weights are better for concentrated training on specific muscles and allow a greater variety of exercises, especially for training specialty muscle groups. The strength training program should be followed three days per week, with a day of rest between each. As you near a major competition, however, reduce the program to two days per week and increase energy training as described later in this chapter.

In designing a strength-training program for karate, you want to target the muscles used for karate motions and effort. Use the correct breathing technique: Exhale as you lift, and inhale as you return to the starting position. Use the full range of motion in all exercises and allow adequate recovery time between sets. Exercise the large muscles before the smaller, more specialized ones, and train antagonist muscles for strength. Vary the less important exercises to avoid boredom, and train different muscle groups on different days. If you use free weights, wear a weight belt for safety.

Variable-Resistance Program. A variable-resistance strength-training program for karate includes leg presses, leg curls, and leg extensions, as well as abdominal crunches and back extensions. These exercises strengthen the lower part of the body. For the upper body, use incline bench presses, biceps curls, lateral pulldowns, rowing, and perhaps deltoid raises. Special exercises such as hip flexion and extensions and triceps extensions can help round out the program.

Free-Weight Program. A free-weight strength-training program includes half squats, leg curls, leg extensions, and heel/toe raises. Bench presses (preferably, inclined), wrist curls, back extensions, and bentover rowing also develop the necessary muscles. Neck flexion and extensions are good supplemental exercises. Exercises that do not use free weights but are excellent additions to this program are curl ups, knuckle pushups, knee lifts, leg raises, and side leg lifts.

Knuckle pushups.

PLYOMETRICS

Plyometric exercises consist of hops, jumps, leaps, skips, rico-chets, swings, and twists. Use them to increase your speed and power. We know that muscles fire faster and more powerfully when they have been preloaded. This is called the elastic recoil action or reflex. Plyometric exercises condition this reflex action, allowing quicker and more powerful changes in direction for attack and defense. Increase your speed and power by reducing movement time. To demonstrate, bend your legs and then leap up into the air. As you land, leap again. The second leap should be easier and higher, taking advantage of the preloading of the muscles that occurs when landing. This is the plyometric effect. This is also demonstrated in the following pictures where you bound back and forth over your partner. Many fighting drills in karate are practiced with the fighter "bouncing" as he moves about. This bouncing preloads the legs for faster movements in attacking or defending. Plyometrics should be performed on days that you are doing your resistance training. Select those exercises that help karate movement. Perform five to six sets of 8-12 repetitions. Keep in mind that the form of the exercise is more important than the quantity.

One plyometric drill is to hop over your partner and then immediately hop back to the other side. This helps create quickness in maneuvering.

CARDIOVASCULAR FITNESS

Karate is a high-energy activity. It requires continuous movement with frequent energy bursts that employ all the major muscle groups and many specialty groups. Energy demands are especially high on the legs and lungs, because these body areas support all explosive actions in karate. A reasonable estimate of energy fitness for karate is 70 percent anaerobic and 30 percent aerobic. Karate practitioners need to build a solid aerobic foundation in order to prepare their respiratory and circulatory systems for rigorous activity.

Aerobic (cardiovascular) fitness is essential for two reasons: to maintain energy levels and to facilitate recovery from anaerobic movement by restoring needed energy supplies. Anaerobic training prepares the body for frequent bursts of intense activity as effort reaches 100 percent. Anaerobic fitness shortens the time needed to recover from intense bursts of energy and raises the "anaerobic threshold"—that point where physical activity changes from aerobic to anaerobic.

The better developed your energy system, the longer you can keep your skills sharp before fatiguing. So, while karate is an excellent training method for energy fitness, other training activities can enhance fitness for karate activities. Two of these activities are jogging and lap swimming. Increase the intensity of your jogging, and add variety, by including rolling terrain or steeper inclines in your route. When swimming or jogging, use intervals of pickup sprints (short bursts of activity above the anaerobic threshold), followed by active rest—periods of less intense movement allowing the body to recover. This type of interval training is discussed below. Other sport activities can also have value for karate practitioners. Racquetball, tennis, soccer, and similar sports require the quick hand-eye or foot-eye coordination that karate requires. They also involve relatively short bursts of all-out energy that are similar to those required in a karate fight. These other fitness activities are helpful if done two to three times a week.

SPEED

In karate, a split instant can make the difference between life and death or winning or losing a match. Flaws in technique also make a critical difference. It has been said, "When speed is vital to performance, speed is part of technique and must be practiced from the beginning" (Knapp, 1964). The idea of speed training is to perform a skill as quickly as possible. Much of speed training involves work on neuromuscular development. The more efficient or highly trained the muscles are, the quicker a movement can be performed. That is why you must perform exercises that develop the crucial muscles used in karate. Speed is improved by

- Practicing at a faster speed than normal, such as using plyometric exercises or running downhill. The faster you practice, the faster you will be in karate competition.
- Reducing the number of tactics choices available. The more varied your tactics, the more difficult it will be to quickly select the right one under pressure.

- Increasing neuromuscular skill through repetition. This creates a highly developed skill. Baseball pitchers throw over a million and a half pitches before reaching the major leagues. As skill increases, advance to 100-percent bursts of speed to reach high-level training.

INTERVAL TRAINING

Interval training is perhaps the best system for karate conditioning. There are a great number of karate drills and exercises that work well for interval training, both with or without a partner. The main advantage of interval training is that you can vary the intensity, duration, and frequency of exercise to get the desired training effect. For example, aerobic interval training uses two- to five-minute intervals of activity with pickups to stimulate the muscles. For anaerobic training, exercise at 90 percent to 95 percent of your potential for intervals not exceeding 90 continuous seconds, followed by an equal period of active rest. Use 100-percent bursts of repetitive motions for high-level speed training. One such interval training may be to sprint for 30 seconds followed by 30 seconds of light jogging. Another may be to punch or kick as fast as possible for one minute followed by a slower pace. One I particularly like is to use a series of punches and strikes and then lightly jog back to the starting point to repeat the series.

CIRCUIT TRAINING

Circuit training can work well with interval training in karate. In circuit training, you perform a number of exercises one after the other for a minimum number of laps or circuits. The number of repetitions for each exercise and the time allowed for each exercise can vary both for the training effect and for progression. If you need to improve your roundhouse kick, for example, you can incorporate exercises such as repeatedly kicking your leg out and back to improve this kick. Plyometrics can help you move more powerfully. Intervals can be adjusted for frequency, duration, and intensity to achieve the desired effect.

To design your program, first decide the number of exercises you wish to incorporate, then determine the duration of each exercise. A well-rounded program includes exercises for strength and endurance, as well as exercising the various muscle groups. The minimum time for completing the given number of circuits is 20 minutes, not including warmup or cooldown.

PUNCHING BOARD AND HEAVY-BAG TRAINING

You cannot be an expert in karate unless you hit. Because of the fierce nature of a karate strike, however, hitting your sparring partners will make them not want to practice with you. Someone may even quit practicing because of fear of injury. Makiwara (punching board) and heavy-bag training provide the means to learn to hit powerfully. This type of training helps the karate-ka coordinate the flow of the muscles in the body with breath and the timing of the blow. Such a combination makes the body an extremely precise and formidable weapon. Use punching board and heavy-bag training for hand and foot attacks, and for blocking actions. This training develops focused power and strengthens those parts of the body you will use as striking weapons.

If you spend a lot of time hitting the punching board and heavy bag, your techniques will become very powerful. You could injure a sparring partner if you don't pull your blows. This type of training is not for children or young adolescents; their bones and joints are not sufficiently developed and could be chronically damaged by hard-hitting activity. Even if your body has reached maturity, improper technique will cause injury.

When starting this type of training, do not hit with full force. Start easy, increasing power as you learn to properly use the hand and foot positions and strengthen the surface of your striking weapon. If you share equipment, consider using bag gloves or tennis shoes. Hands and feet are commonly cut or scratched by the striking surface, and you do not want to leave bloody marks or pieces of the skin on the equipment.

When hitting the punching board or heavy bag, move the large muscles of your body first. Align the connections and tense the body sharply, releasing a loud kiai at the moment of impact. Strike at the correct angle so that the entire force of the blow goes into the target. Do not target the surface of the punching board or heavy bag, but aim the blow into the target for maximum penetration.

Heavy bag training is excellent for developing strong kicks.

Training with the punching board will develop power.

Having the skills to defend yourself is one thing, but being able to carry out that defense in the grueling reality of a life-or-death situation or a competition is another. Enhancing your karate training with flexibility, strength, aerobic, heavy bag, and makiwara training will let you hone your body into a fine fighting tool, put you in great shape, and add healthy years to your life expectancy in the process.

SUGGESTED READINGS

Anderson, G.E. 1976. *Kwanmukan manual.* Akron: Kwanmukan Mudo Association.

Atha, J. 1981. Strengthening muscle. *Exercise and Sport Science Reviews* 9:1-73.

deVries, H.A. 1986. *Physiology of exercise.* 4th ed. Dubuque, IA: Brown.

Egami, Shigeru. 1976. *The way of karate: Beyond technique.* Tokyo: Kodansha International.

Fleck, J.S., and W.J. Kraemer. 1987. *Designing resistance training programs.* Champaign, IL: Human Kinetics.

Funakoshi, G. 1975. *Karate-do, my way of life.* Tokyo: Kodansha International.

————. 1973. *Karate-do kyohan: The master text.* Tokyo: Kodansha International.

Hickey, P.M. 1993. *Kwanmukan book 5: Elite karate training: Competition.* Akron, Ohio: Kwanmukan International.

————. P. M. (October, 1992). Enhancing your karate training. *Karate Kung Fu Illustrated,* 8-13.

————. P.M., ed. 1985. *The USA Karate Federation national referee course notebook.* Akron, OH: USA Karate of Ohio.

————. P.M. (January, 1984). WUKO holds First Technical Congress. *Karate Illustrated.*

————. P.M. (May, 1983). An American's view of kata competition. *Combat,* 38-40.

————. P.M. (March, 1983). A traditionalist looks at modern kata competition. *Karate Illustrated,* 44-45, 74-75.

Illustrated kodokan judo. 1955. Tokyo: Kodansha International Ltd.

Kanazawa, H. 1983. *Shotokan Karate International: Kata.* Vol. 1. Tokyo: Shotokan Karate International.

————. 1983. *Shotokan Karate International: Kata.* Vol. 2. Tokyo: Shotokan Karate International.

Knapp, B. 1964. *Skill in sport: The attainment of proficiency.* London: Routledge & Kegan Paul.

Komi, P. 1986. The stretch shortening cycle and human power output. In *Human Muscle Power,* edited by N.L. Jones, N. McCartney, and A.J. McComas, 27-40. Champaign, IL: Human Kinetics.

Shotokan karate by T. Mikami. 1986. Anderson/Hickey Productions. Videocassette.

Nagamine, S. 1976. *The essence of Okinawan karate-do.* Tokyo: Charles E. Tuttle.

Nakayama, M. 1981. *Best karate: Comprehensive—1.* Tokyo: Kodansha International/USA.

————. 1981. *Best karate: Fundamentals—2.* Tokyo: Kodansha International/USA.

————. 1981. *Best karate: Kumite 1—3.* Tokyo: Kodansha International/USA.

————. 1981. *Best karate: Kumite 2—4.* Tokyo: Kodansha International/USA.

————. 1968. *Karate kata: Heian 4.* Tokyo: Kodansha International.

————. 1966. *Dynamic karate.* Tokyo: Kodansha International.

Nishiyama, H., and R.C. Brown. 1959. *Karate: The art of empty hand fighting.* Tokyo: Charles E. Tuttle.

Ratti, O., and A. Westbrook. 1973. *Secrets of the samurai.* Tokyo: Charles E. Tuttle.

Sharkey, B.J. 1990. *Physiology of fitness.* 3d ed. Champaign, IL: Human Kinetics.

————. 1986. *Coaches guide to sport physiology.* Champaign, IL: Human Kinetics.

Sugiyama, S. 1984. *Twenty-five shoto-kan kata.* Chicago: Shojiro Sugiyama.

Sugiyama, S. and his students. 1977. *Karate: Synchronization of body and mind.* Chicago: Shojiro Sugiyama.

Suzuki, T. 1984. *Karate-do.* New York: Perigee Books.

Toguchi, S. 1976. *Okinawan goju-ryu.* Los Angeles: Ohara.

Tohei, K. 1973. *What is aikido?* Japan: Rikugie.

Tomiki, K. 1961. *Judo and aikido.* Japan: Japan Travel Bureau.

Yamaguchi, G. 1974. Goju-ryu karate II. Los Angeles: Ohara.

————. 1972. *The fundamentals of goju-ryu karate.* Los Angeles: Ohara.

INDEX

A

Abdomen, 56, 103, 106, 108, 114, 118, 157, 174
Advancement, 9, 10-12, 151. *See also* Belt testing
Aikido, 5, 200
Aiki-jitsu, 5
Atemi, 77, 176. *See also* Punching
Attacker (uke), 27
Attacks
    angle of, 98, 132
    as blocks, 68
    blocks as attacks, 68
    breakdown, 148
    circular, 132
    direct, 132
    foot, 128, 196
    hand, 78, 88
    indirect, 132
    moment of, 130
    openings, 135
    simultaneous attack, 68
    straight-in, 132
    taking the initiative, 128, 136

B

Balance, 51, 52, 54, 57, 58, 103, 128, 156, 161, 162
Belt ranking, *See* Advancement; Belt testing
Belt testing, 7, 11, 128, 142, 151, 154
Black belt, 7, 9, 11, 12, 22, 30, 32, 88
Blocking, 57-70, 127, 131, 136, 139, 155
    basic blocks, 58, 59
    blocks as attacks, 68
    blocks with feet, 69-70
    direct blocking, 68
    double block, 67
    downward block (low sweeping block), 59, 63, 67
    inside-outside block, 59, 62
    knife-hand block, 64, 67
    outside-inside block, 59, 61, 67
    simultaneous attack, 68-69
    simultaneous block, 68-69
    strikes as blocks, 88
    supporting block, 65
    sword-arm block, 64
    two-handed/supporting block, 65
    upper block (rising block), 59, 60
    wedge block, 67
Bow, 25, 28, 160, 169
Breaking balance, 137
Breathing, 33, 34, 52, 55-56, 58, 78, 191
    ibuki, 56
    in kata, 152-156
    kiai, 25, 56, 78, 89, 105, 157, 176, 196
    nogare, 56
Budo, 17, 18
Bunkai. *See* Kata

C

Cardiovascular fitness, 185, 193
China, 4, 13, 14
Closure, theory of, 128, 134, 148
Competition, 172. *See also* Kata competition;
    Kumite competition
    preparation for, 183
    international, 16-19
    strategy for. *See* Strategy
    tactics for. *See* Tactics
Conditioning. *See also* Strength training
    aerobic fitness, 2, 28, 193, 195, 198
    anaerobic fitness, 193, 194
    cardiovascular fitness, 185, 193
    circuit training, 185, 195
    diet, 183
    endurance, 148, 185, 190, 196
    exercise, 151, 186, 187, 195
    exercise equipment, 7
    fighting weight, 183
    fitness, 12, 14, 190, 191, 193, 194
    flexibility, 102, 128, 136, 151, 157, 183, 185
    flexibility exercises, 186-189
    interval training, 185, 194, 195
    plyometric exercises, 185, 192-193
    power. *See* Strength training
    seasonal training, 182-184
    speed, 51, 89, 103, 125, 128, 176
    speed training, 185, 191, 194, 195
    stretching, 28, 186
    training, 183, 185, 191, 192, 194, 195
    warm-ups, 28, 186
Controlling the opponent, 149
Cool-down, 28, 186
Counting, 25

D

Deai-waza, 130
Defender (tori), 27
Defends. *See* Blocking
Diaphragm, 52, 55, 56
Discipline, 1, 2, 6, 151
Distance, 77, 134, 152, 173, 176

Do (way), 15
Dojo (training hall), 22

E

Eku. *See* Kata
Exercise, 151, 186, 187, 195. *See also* Conditioning

F

Falls, 70-71
Fatigue, 148
Fighting position, 48, 128, 134
Fitness, 12, 14, 190, 191, 193, 194
Flexibility, 102, 128, 136, 151, 157, 183, 185
Form (katachi). *See* Kata
Free fighting. *See* Kumite
Fumi-dashi, 55

G

Gaze, 47, 128, 130, 152, 156, 158
Gi, 22, 24, 159, 160, 165
Guard position, 47-48, 50, 83, 129
    fighting guard, 129
    high guard, 50, 129
    low guard, 49, 129
    middle guard, 48, 49, 128, 129
Gyaku kaiten, 52

H

Hand position, 48, 58, 66, 125
    knife-hand, 64
    other positions, 93
    punching, 78, 79
    striking, 88
Hara, 52, 158, 174, 176
Heavy bag, 7, 185, 196, 198
Hips
    dynamic stability, 54
    movement of, 52
    turning, 51
    twisting, 52, 84

I

Injury prevention
    in competition, 165, 175, 178
    in practice, 27, 136
Ippon, 17
    competition standard, 169, 172, 173, 174
    criteria for, 175-178
    penalty, 182

J

Japan, 3, 15-16, 127, 159
Japanese pronunciation, 21, 22
Japanese vocabulary, 29-32
Judo, 4, 5, 8, 9
Jujitsu, 4, 5, 7, 9
Jun kaiten, 52

K

Kama. *See* Kata
Kamae (upper body position), 47, 78, 139
    natural body positions, 37-38. *See also* Stances
    natural body posture, 22, 29, 37
    reverse side-facing, 34

side-facing, 34, 46, 51, 83, 84, 128, 129
Karate
    class, 5, 12, 22, 24-28
    competition. *See* Kata competition; Kumite
        competition
    customs of, 12, 21, 23, 24, 29
    definition of, 3
    development of, 14
    founders of, 15, 19, 127, 157, 199
    general forms of, 22-23
    history of, 13-18
    pronunciation, 21, 22
    styles of, 3, 4, 19, 20, 22
    training terms, 25
    uniform (gi), 22, 24, 159, 165, 180
    vocabulary, 21, 29-32
Karate school
    finding, 3
    selecting, 1, 6-8
Kata, 26, 28, 151-162
    bassai dai, 153
    belt advancement, 151, 154
    breathing, 156
    cardinal rules, 157
    characteristics, 156
    embussen (line of kata movement), 156
    interpretation, 26, 151, 152, 156, 157
    movement, 154, 155, 157
    seishan, 154
    understanding, 151
    weapons kata, 154, 158, 162
    weapons, 14, 136, 159
Kata competition, 158-162, 199
    conducting competition, 159, 160
    rules for, 158-162
    scoring, 160-162
    team divisions (synchronized kata), 158
Kawashi (dodging), 127, 143, 150
Kendo, 5
Ki (spirit), 5
Kiai, 25, 56, 78, 89, 105, 157, 176, 196
Kicking, 5, 28, 34, 78, 101-119
    axe kick, 117
    back kick, 101, 103, 112-113, 116
    chambering, 104, 118, 125
    crescent kick, 69, 101, 102, 103, 104, 114-115,
        117
    double kick, 117, 140
    front kick, 52, 69, 77, 101, 103, 106-107, 117
    high kicks, 102
    hook kick, 117, 140
    in competition, 172, 177, 179
    in self-defense, 118-119
    jump kick, 116
    pivoting, 51, 108, 110, 112, 124, 140, 149
    reverse crescent kick, 114-115
    roundhouse kick, 101, 103, 108-109, 116, 117,
        124
    side kick, 101, 102, 103, 110-111, 112, 116, 117
    snap kick, 102, 103, 106, 110
    spin kick, 117
    striking surfaces, 102
    thrust kick, 102, 103, 106, 110
    use in tactics and strategy 132, 133, 135, 139,
        148, 140
    wheel kick, 117, 172
Kihon (basics), 11, 176

attacking leg, 51
center of gravity, 54, 84, 137, 156, 158
connections, 51, 56, 196
driving leg, 51, 54, 55
kata, 26, 28
kumite, 135, 136
moving leg, 51, 54, 55
posture, 11, 24, 34, 37, 47, 52, 128
pivot leg, 51
reaction force, 52
side-facing, 34, 63, 83, 84
side-stepping, 45
withdrawing hand, 52, 54, 78, 83, 120
Kime, 174
Kobudo. See Kata, weapons
Korea, 3, 4, 9
Kumite, 26, 27. See also Kumite competition;
    Strategy; Tactics
ippon, 27, 135, 136, 152
one step, 27, 135, 136, 152
prearranged, 11
semi-free, 135, 136, 183
sparring, 135
Karate competition. See Kata competition;
    Kumite competition
Kumite competition, 163-184
breaking a tie, 169, 172
competition ring, 164, 166
conducting the match, 169, 170, 172, 175
duration, 169
in bounds, 175
injury, 165, 166, 171, 175, 179, 180
ippon shobu, 17
judging system, 16, 166
match time, 166, 174
mubobi, 179, 180, 182
officials
    in kata, 158, 160, 161, 162
    in kumite, 166, 169, 181-182
out-of-bounds, 165, 170, 175, 179, 180
penalties, 171, 174, 175, 178, 179, 181, 182
preparation, 182
prohibited behavior, 178-181
protective equipment, 165
referee commands, 167-168
rules, 4, 16, 172-181
scoring, criteria for, 175-177
scoring technique, 170, 174, 175, 177
shobu sanbon, 17, 169
target areas, 106, 173, 174
warning zone, 164
Kyu. See Belt ranking; Belt testing

L

Law enforcement, 5, 7
Lotus position, 55

M

Maai. See Distancing, 134, 176
Meditation, 14, 24, 26, 28, 55, 183. See also
    Breathing; Mokuso
Mobility, 34, 128
Mokuso (meditation), 24, 55

N

Natural body positions. See Stances

Natural body posture, 22, 29, 37. See also Kamae
Nunchaku. See Kata, weapons

O

Okinawa, 3, 5, 14, 15
Olympics, 4, 14, 18, 19, 20
Organizations
in Japan, 16, 19
international, 16-20, 159, 165, 172, 173, 177
sports, 15, 18, 20
US karate, 16, 20

P

Posture
in fighting, 129
in kata, 154, 161
in kumite, 177
in stances, 47, 52
Power
in kata, 158
in kicks, 103
in kumite, 176
in stances, 51, 52, 54
power training. See Strength training
Punching, 54, 77, 78-88, 98, 132, 195
alternate punch, 88
basic punch, 82-83
both-hands punch, 88
"close" punch, 83
double punch, 31, 88
flat fist/fore-knuckle fist, 81
forefist, 52, 79
hiraken (flat fist), 81, 82
hooking punch, 83
ippon-ken (middle knuckle fist), 81
lunge punch, 86-87
nakadaka-ken (middle finger one-knuckle fist),
    81, 82
parallel punch, 88
reverse punch, 34, 84
rising punch, 83
roundhouse punch, 83
scissors punch, 88
straight punch, 34, 84-85
upper jab, 83
upper punch, 83
upward punch, 83
vertical punch, 83
wide U-punch, arms apart (mountain strike),
    83
Punching board, 185, 196

R

Ranging, 134, 173
Retraction, 103, 117
Rolls, 70-71
rolling backward, 74-75
rolling forward, 72-73

S

Sai. See Kata, weapons
Seishan. See Kata
Self-defense, 28, 101, 117, 120
Self-defense tips, 68, 98, 118, 149
Sensei, 22, 23, 24
Sitting (seiza), 24

Smashes, 78, 102, 120-125
    elbow smash, 118, 120-123, 125
    knee smash, 101, 120, 124-125
Stability, 34, 51, 54, 77
Stances, 28, 34-46
    advantages of, 36
    back stance, 34, 36, 40, 128
    cat stance, 34, 36, 44, 83, 102, 128
    changing, 54
    disadvantages of, 36
    fighting stance, 27, 37, 41, 128
    fixed stance, 46
    front stance, 36, 39, 46, 128
    hourglass stance, 42
    moving, 51
    natural body positions, 37-38
        attention stance, 37, 38
        L-stance, 37, 38
        open-leg stance, 27, 37
        parallel stance, 37, 38
        T-stance, 37, 38
    pivoting, 51, 54
    reverse stance, 34-35
    rooted stance, 46
    square or sumo stance, 43
    straddle-leg stance, 36, 41, 43, 46, 110
    straight stance, 34-35
    sumo stance, 43
    X-stance, 36, 45
Strategy, 127-134, 142, 146, 158
    danger zone, 132, 133, 134
    defensive sphere, 134
    defensive zone, 58, 132, 133, 134
    escape, 128, 134, 146, 149, 150, 180
    escape zone, 132, 133
    mental or physical moment, 130-131
    safety zone, 128, 132
    taking the initiative, 130
Street-fighting, 139
Strength training, 7, 185, 190, 191. See also Con-
        ditioning
    for power, 185, 190, 192, 196
    free weights, 185, 190, 191
    muscle strength, 183
    muscular fitness, 190
    variable-resistance, 185, 190, 191
    weights, 7, 185, 190, 191
Stretching, 28, 186. See also Conditioning
Striking, 52, 77-78, 88-99, 132, 195
    backfist strike, 88, 92, 93, 98-99
    backhand strike, 93, 94
    bear-hand strike, 94, 97
    bent-wrist strike, 94, 97
    chicken-wrist strike, 94, 96
    eagle-hand strike, 94, 98
    hammer-fist strike/bottom fist, 88, 93, 98
    inside circular strike, 88
    knife-hand strike, 47, 64, 88, 90-91, 98-99
    outside circular strike, 88

    ox-jaw strike, 94, 96
    palm-heel strike, 94, 95, 98
    ridge-hand strike, 93, 95, 98
    sideways strike, 88
    spear hand, 78, 80
    vertical strike, 88
Striking surfaces, 79, 92, 93, 94, 102, 108, 120, 196

T

Tactics, 134-147, 148, 149, 173, 194
    body shifting (tai sabaki), 137, 143, 149
    breaking the balance, 137-139
    developing, 135-137
    double kicking, 139, 140-141
    faking, 117, 135, 139, 171, 180
    hit-move-hit, 143-145
    kuzushi, 137
    leg sweeping, 137
    off-balancing, 137, 154
    pattern attacks, 142, 146-148
    pressuring the opponent, 142
    takedowns, 137
Taekwondo, 3, 4
Technique. See Kihon (basics)
Throwing, 72, 73, 86, 128, 137, 195
Timing, 27, 33, 134, 136
    in kata, 152, 153, 154, 158
    in kumite, 176
Tonfa. See Kata, weapons
To-te, 13, 14

U

United States, 3, 4, 13, 16, 17, 19, 20
Upper-body position, 47, 78, 139. See also Kamae

V

Vital strike (atemi), 77, 153, 176
Vocabulary, 29-32

W

Waza, 26, 28, 130
Waza-ari, 169, 172, 174, 175, 176, 177, 178
    criteria for, 175-178
    in practice, 169, 172, 173
Weapons. See Kata, weapons
World championships, 19
World Technical Congress, 16-17
Wu Shu, 4

Y

Yori-ashi, 55

Z

Zanshin, 47, 152, 156, 157, 176, 177
Zen, 15, 22

ABOUT THE AUTHOR

Patrick M. Hickey is a seventh-dan black belt in karate who has more than 25 years of experience as a competitor, instructor, referee, and judge. He is also a certified black belt in judo, jujitsu, and kobudo. Hickey is a former Amateur Athletic Union (AAU) karate officer, a nationally rated referee since 1979, and an internationally rated referee since 1984. An officer for the U.S. national governing body for karate from 1986 to 1994, Hickey also was a director of the U.S. Karate Association's Law Enforcement Division, heading this group that certifies instructors who teach karate to law enforcement personnel. He has served as a referee, chief referee, or judge for many national and international competitions. Having been the Referee Certification Chairman for both the USA Karate Federation and AAU Karate, Hickey has also been the Coach Certification Chairman for the USA Karate Federation. He helped develop the rules of the World Karate Federation.

Hickey lives in Stow, Ohio, with his wife, Pamela. In addition to his avid involvement with martial arts, he likes to play guitar and enjoys sailing and playing on a soccer team.